"Learning to  us in an entertaining way. From chapter to chapter we were inspired to examine our relationship and measure it against biblical principles for marriage. We need Pastor Henry's light-hearted but poignant teaching in a society where living together before marriage seems to be acceptable, the divorce rate is high, and happily married couples appear to be in the minority."

Ralph and Gail Eichler,
Manitoba Legislature

"Marriage is serious business. *Knot Happy* is serious business done well with a good sense of humor. Dr. Ozirney draws on over thirty years of experience as husband and pastor to provide biblical guidance for the covenant of marriage. Snappy chapters concluding with thoughtful questions will enable every married couple to improve their relationship, and will guide those planning marriage to make a life-long relationship both good and happy."

August H. Konkel
Providence Theological Seminary

"*Knot Happy* is a true reflection of Henry's adventure in making his journey with Linda work. The challenges presented in marriage and divorce will greatly benefit small study groups and individuals. This is a must for your personal library."

Tim Treadway,
Pioneer Quest and husband for 32 years

"Replete with anecdotal wisdom and Henry's jokes, *Knot Happy's* credibility lies in the simple fact that the after 35 years of marriage, he is adored by his wife and children. While reading the manuscript, I was several times compelled to put it down and do something random, affectionate, and kind for my wife and kids."

Steve Bell,
Singer/Songwriter

KNOT ✸ HAPPY

HOW YOUR MARRIAGE **CAN** BE

KNOT ✳ HAPPY

HOW YOUR MARRIAGE CAN BE

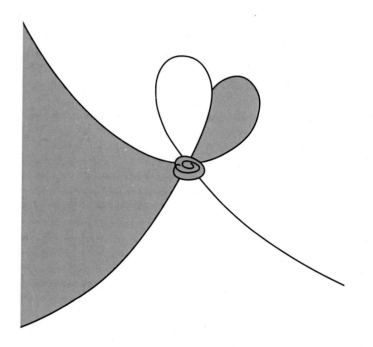

DR. HENRY A. OZIRNEY

Tate Publishing & *Enterprises*

Tate Publishing
& Enterprises

Tate Publishing is committed to excellence in the publishing industry. Our staff of highly trained professionals, including editors, graphic designers, and marketing personnel, work together to produce the very finest books available. The company reflects the philosophy established by the founders, based on Psalms 68:11,

"The Lord Gave The Word And Great Was The Company Of Those Who Published It."

If you would like further information, please contact us:
1.888.361.9473 | www.tatepublishing.com
Tate Publishing & *Enterprises*, LLC | 127 E. Trade Center Terrace
Mustang, Oklahoma 73064 USA

Knot Happy—How Your Marriage Can Be
Copyright © 2007 by Dr. Henry A. Ozirney. All rights reserved.
This title is also available as a Tate Out Loud product.
Visit www.tatepublishing.com for more information

No part of this publication may be reproduced, stored in a retrieval system or transmitted in any way by any means, electronic, mechanical, photocopy, recording or otherwise without the prior permission of the author except as provided by USA copyright law.

No part of this publication may be reproduced, stored in a retrieval system or transmitted in any way by any means, electronic, mechanical, photocopy, recording or otherwise without the prior permission of the author except as provided by USA copyright law.

Scripture quotations marked "cev" are from the *Holy Bible; Contemporary English Version*, Copyright © 1995, Barclay M. Newman, ed., American Bible Society. Used by permission. All rights reserved.

Scripture quotations marked "kjv" are taken from the *Holy Bible, King James Version*, Cambridge, 1769. Used by permission. All rights reserved.

Scripture quotations marked "Msg" are taken from *The Message*, Copyright © 1993, 1994, 1995, 1996, 2000, 2001, 2002. Used by permission of NavPress Publishing Group. All rights reserved.

Scripture quotations marked "nas" are taken from the *New American Standard Bible* ®, Copyright © 1960, 1962, 1963, 1968, 1971, 1972, 1973, 1975, 1977, 1995 by The Lockman Foundation. Used by permission. All rights reserved.

Scripture quotations marked "ncv" are taken from the *Holy Bible, The New Century Version* ®, Copyright © 1987, 1988, 1991. Used by permission of Word Publishing. All rights reserved.

Scripture quotations not marked are taken from the *Holy Bible, New International Version* ®, Copyright © 1973, 1978, 1984 by International Bible Society. Used by permission of Zondervan Publishing House. All rights reserved.

Scripture quotations marked "nlt" are taken from the *Holy Bible, New Living Translation,* Copyright © 1996. Used by permission of Tyndale House Publishers, Inc. All rights reserved.

Scripture quotations marked "Ph" are taken from *The New Testament in Modern English,* Copyright © 1958, 1959, 1960 J.B. Phillips and 1947, 1952, 1955, 1957 The Macmillian Company, New York. Used by permission. All rights reserved.

Scripture quotations marked "tlb" are taken from *The Living Bible* / Kenneth N. Taylor: Tyndale House, © Copyright 1997, 1971 by Tyndale House Publishers, Inc. Used by permission. All rights reserved.

The opinions expressed by the author are not necessarily those of Tate Publishing, LLC.

This book is designed to provide accurate and authoritative information with regard to the subject matter covered. This information is given with the understanding that neither the author nor Tate Publishing, LLC is engaged in rendering legal, professional advice. Since the details of your situation are fact dependent, you should additionally seek the services of a competent professional.

The opinions expressed by the author are not necessarily those of Tate Publishing, LLC.

Book design copyright © 2007 by Tate Publishing, LLC. All rights reserved.
Cover design by Leah LeFlore
Interior design by Elizabeth A. Mason

Published in the United States of America

ISBN: 978-1-60247-364-5
07.03.12

To my precious wife, Linda, with whom I tied the knot 35 years ago and with whom I have experienced the happiness I write about. Thank you for believing in me that I could write a book. I will never forget the day about 20 years ago when you came home with a notebook you had purchased for me, in which you had written, "Dearest Henry, I have known you for 18 years and lived with you for almost 14 years so I think I know you quite well by now...And I really believe you have the qualifications for an author...So I bought you this scribbler for you to start a rough draft of your first published book. I love you and will pray for you that thoughts will come to you and this book will really become a reality. So go for it Henry...for God's glory!"

This book is the result of all your encouragement over the years, sweetheart.

And to Craig and Carena, Evan and Eric, Curtis, Kristyn and Kevin, Nathan (and the new baby on the way!) and Kent and Florence. You are the joy of my life. You make our family the great thing that it is.

ACKNOWLEDGMENTS

I want to thank the following people who have helped make this book a possibility:

Lenore Oakford who responded to my request for help with the editing and did such a super job! Thanks, also, Doug for giving up your time with Lenore so she could do this.

Lisa Chlysta and Rudy Giesbrecht who helped me with researching the best way to publish this book and gave invaluable counsel.

My children, Craig and his wife Carena, Kristyn and her husband Kevin, Kent and his wife Florence, my sister Natalie James, as well as Brenda Bawden, Al Hickey, Lisa Chlysta and Lynne Friesen who proof read the manuscript and made helpful suggestions.

Our church secretary, Joelle Newman, who helped me out in so many different ways, as she always does.

The rest of our entire church office staff who were so supportive and helpful: Associate Pastor Glenn

Miller; Susie Schwartz, Director of Youth Ministries; and Terri Houdayer, Director of Children's Ministries.

The Promise Keeper's group of our church who made the commitment to give a gift of the book, when it is published, to each family in our church.

And, of course, to the wonderful church that I have had the amazing privilege of serving as the pastor for the past 37 years. They were frequently my teachers in many of the truths found in these pages. They have listened to hundreds and hundreds of my sermons and have always been so supportive. This book is based on a series of messages given in the church in the fall of 2002, and it was their initial encouragement that I should put these messages into a book that got me going in this direction. It was also their decision to grant me a sabbatical in the summer of 2006 that enabled me to get this book written. I will forever be in your debt.

In preparation for those messages in 2002, I also found a series of messages from Rick Warren, pastor of Saddleback Church in southern California, to be immensely helpful and have used his ideas liberally, especially in chapters 9, 10, 11, and 13. Thanks, Rick, for giving me permission to use it to help people's marriages. Those ideas *had* to be in print.

And, of course, thank you to my wife, Linda. She is one very amazing woman. It is because of her that this book is a reality, in more ways than one.

Finally, thank you to Jesus, who made everything possible in the first place. I love you, Jesus.

CONTENTS

Foreword	13
Introduction	15
Marriage, By Definition	17
Come Hell or High-water	29
How to be Happy Though Married	43
What is Love?	65
This, My Dear, is How I Love You!	81
More Joy in Your Marriage	97
Sex and the Christian Couple	113
In-Laws and Other Outlaws	131
How Come There's So Much Month at the End of the Money?	145
Fight the Good Fight	165
A Marriage Makeover	187
Till Divorce Parts Us	197
When Your Heart is Breaking: The End of a Marriage	217
Keeping the Home Fires Burning	237
Epilogue	249

FOREWORD

Marriage is always under scrutiny by societies. It can be ridiculed or celebrated, mocked or encouraged, criticized yet embraced by the majority. Marriages have the potential to bring amazing and meaningful relationships to us. Most young people are still growing up with a deep longing to be married and raise a family.

When my parents married, they pledged their vows before God with a pastor and two witnesses in the home of a friend. Weddings today are big business, with the average wedding in the United States costing $25,000. The entertainment business is also reaping huge profits, marketing perfect weddings on reality TV.

We understand innately, that marriage is much more than a wedding, yet most couples continue to give an inordinate amount of time to wedding planning and budgeting. Too little energy and thought is given in preparing for a satisfying and rewarding life-long marriage. It is customary for us to spend years preparing and educating ourselves for a successful career, and yet we delegate the future happiness and security of the most important institution in the world to emotional responses and movie inspired romance.

In *Knot Happy–How Your Marriage Can Be,* Dr. Henry Ozirney has given us a practical outline on how to build a successful marriage. His life-long ministry in one church community has provided him with ample case studies on how to nurture a successful marriage or conversely to design its demise. My role as an associate pastor with Dr. Ozirney for the past twelve years has given me opportunity to observe that he is a student of his own teaching on this critical subject.

You will chuckle and identify with the humorous antidotes and be instructed by the practical biblical teaching that can help rearrange your marriage into a healthy and happy one. The questions at the end of each chapter are designed to assist small groups grapple with the teaching provided in the chapter. Whether you are a novice or a veteran in marriage, you will benefit from reading and following the advice given in this handbook.

Read digest, and enjoy the renewal and bolstering your marriage will receive and pass along the practical advice to others who are facing the same challenges in their journey of oneness.

Rev. Glenn Miller, M.A.
New Life Church
Stonewall, MB

INTRODUCTION

She had just about reached her limit. After five years of marriage to him, she felt she could not continue on. For the past couple of years, she had often awoken in the middle of the night, unable to sleep. She would get into the car and drive around town. It was her way of retaining her sanity in a very unhappy marriage.

Often, she contemplated simply driving and never returning. One afternoon, with her young son in the car, she decided to keep on driving instead of returning home after her errand was complete. But, she realized she could not. She had an infant son who she could not care for on her own. So she returned home, resigned to spending the rest of her life in a very unhappy marriage.

Her husband, in the meantime, was totally oblivious to this. He did not realize how desperate things were. It wasn't until many years later, when she told him what she had almost done, that he realized the seriousness of their marital problems at the time.

That husband is me and the woman, who almost

drove out of my life 30 years ago, is my lovely wife, Linda, with whom I celebrated our 35th anniversary this past July. This book is the result of some of the lessons I have since learned on how to have a truly happy marriage.

It is still popular to use the terminology, "tie the knot", to refer to being united in holy matrimony. This idiom comes from days gone by when bed frames used to be sprung with rope. To make a marriage bed, one needed to "tie the knot."[1] Even today, in some marriage ceremonies, the officiating minister will tie together the wrists of both the bride and groom.

When Linda and I tied the knot, we both were hoping it would be a happy union. As I have already shared, it was not happy at first. But the good news is that, through the grace of God, we moved from "not happy" to "knot happy."

This book shows the Biblical principles that have given us marital satisfaction that I call "knot happy." As a matter a fact, I am so totally convinced that any couple who will both study together and completely follow the Biblical teachings in this book, I will guarantee them that, not only will they never divorce, but they *will* be "knot happy"! (And that's a "money-back guarantee"!)

Dr. Henry A. Ozirney,
February 28, 2007

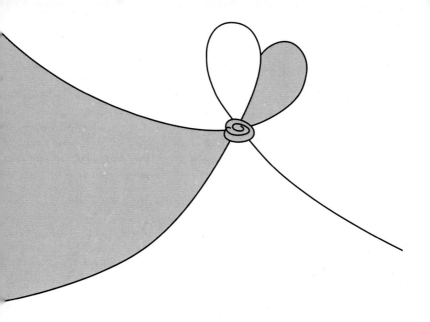

MARRIAGE, BY DEFINITION

It had been a great banquet that my wife Linda and I, accompanied by our friends, Howard and Caron, had just attended. Everyone was leaving the banquet hall at the same time and with 800 or so people all going for the same exit, there was quite a crush of people. Always on the lookout for the quickest way out, I was pleased to see a gap in the crowd. I remember thinking, *If we go that way, we can be out of here in no time at all.*

So, with my eyes fastened on that route, I reached out for Linda and pulled her to my side. As I did, and my hand touched her dress, I thought, *Hmmm...This material is different from that of the dress she came to the banquet in...*

Slowly, I shifted my eyes to my side and realized I had my arm around a woman I had never seen before.

Glancing behind her, I could see a man I had never seen before either, and the expression on his face was none too happy. Obviously, as the husband, he was not overly impressed by my friendliness with his wife. What do you do when you're in a situation like that? You do some fast thinking!

So, I pretended I was an usher. With my hand still on the woman's back, I pointed out the path I was going to take and said, "This way, ma'am..." as I pushed her forward. Then I put my hand behind her husband's back and instructed him to follow his wife.

At that point, I looked back at Linda, Howard, and Caron and saw them doubled over in laughter. It wasn't until later that evening that I was able to join them in laughing at the mess I had gotten myself into. In the same way, a lot of people's marriages are in a mess. Too many people, it seems, are not happy in their marriage.

At the same time, there is also a great confusion in much of today's society as to what marriage is all about. That confusion is typified by the nine-year-old boy who was asked by his Sunday School teacher, "What did Jesus say to the couple at the wedding of Cana in Galilee?" He responded, "He said to them, 'Father, forgive them for they do not know what they are doing.'"

WHAT IS MARRIAGE?

Just what is marriage? I once heard someone suggest that it is an institution held together by two books: cook and cheque. Someone else said that marriage is like a ways and means committee: she directs the ways and he furnishes the means. Ogden Nash offered his definition in his poem, "I Do, I Will, I Have."

> I am about to volunteer a definition of marriage./ Just as I know that there are two Hagens, Walter and Copen,/ I know that marriage is a legal and religious alliance entered into by a man who can't sleep with the window shut and a woman who can't sleep with the window open./ Moreover, just as I am unsure of the difference between flora and fauna and flotsam and jetsam,/ I am quite sure that marriage is the alliance of two people one of whom never remembers birthdays and the other never forgetsam,/ And he refuses to believe there is a leak in the water pipe or the gas pipe and she is convinced she is about to asphyxiate or drown,/ And she says Quick get up and get my hairbrushes off the windowsill, it's raining in, and he replies Oh they're alright, it's only raining straight down./ That is why marriage is so much more interesting than divorce,/ Because it's the only known example of the happy meeting of the immovable object and the irresistible force./ So I hope husbands and wives will continue to debate and combat over everything debatable and combatable,/ Because I believe a little incompatibility is the spice of life, particularly if he has income and she is pattable.[2]

However, the definition of marriage is a bit more complicated in Canada. I was in the House of Commons in

Ottawa, in June 2000, when a debate on the definition of marriage was being held. I listened to the arguments, pro and con, for same sex marriage. At that time, the vote to retain the definition of marriage to be a "lawful union of one man and one woman to the exclusion of all others" passed. However, just five years later, in 2005, the Canadian government, in its Civil Marriage Act, voted into law that "marriage, for civil purposes, is the lawful union of two persons to the exclusion of all others."[3] As a result, they ruled that people of the same sex could be married, just as two people of the opposite sex previously had been.

Many people in Canada opposed this vote and many others seemed confused by all of this. In light of so much confusion, my question is: What does God say about marriage? What does the Bible teach? That is what I want to know. It is my firm conviction that that is where we must begin.

Let me tell you a story to illustrate why I begin there. A man was driving down the road in a brand new Model 'A' Ford that he had just bought, and like many Fords are still prone to do, it stopped. I say that, but I must confess that I do love the 1966 Ford Mustang that I bought and restored recently. As he was trying to get it going, another Model 'A' Ford came by and a man got out. He looked at the motor, did this and that, and the car started immediately. The new owner was pleased and thanked the man for fixing it. It turned out the mechanic was none other than Henry Ford, the inventor of the car.

So also, marriage works best and people are happiest in it when they follow the blueprint laid out by marriage's inventor, God. If the inventor says this is how this machine is supposed to work, then I want to follow his guidance, not that of someone who didn't come up with the idea and knows very little about it. The Bible is our marriage manual.

As one studies the scripture, two concepts arise that describe marriage. A look now at both of these:

A COVENANT

According to the Bible, marriage is a formal contract between a man and woman. In Proverbs 2:16–17, we read, "It (the teachings of God's word) will save you also from the adulteress, from the wayward wife with her seductive words, who has left the partner of her youth and *ignored the covenant she made before God.*" According to this scripture, leaving one's spouse for another is ignoring a covenant made before God.

In Ezekiel 16:8, God used the marriage union as an illustration of His own relationship to the nation Israel:

> Later I passed by, and when I looked at you and saw that you were old enough for love, I spread the corner of my garment over you and covered your nakedness. *I gave you my solemn oath and entered into a covenant with you,* declares the Sovereign LORD, and you became mine.

God entered into a contract with His chosen people, the Israelites, and in the same way, a husband enters into a contract with his wife when he marries her.

The prophet Malachi described God's anger at Israel's unfaithfulness by their casual disregard of their marriage commitments:

> Another thing you do: You flood the Lord's altar with tears. You weep and wail because he no longer pays attention to your offerings or accepts them with pleasure from your hands. You ask, "Why?" It is because the Lord is acting as the witness between you and the wife of your youth, because you have broken faith with her, *though she is your partner, the wife of your marriage covenant.* (Malachi 2:13–14)

God's rejection of the Israelite's offerings was because they were not keeping their marriage vows with their wives.

Each of these scriptures uses the word "covenant" to describe how one enters into a marriage relationship. Why a covenant, a contract? It is because God sees marriage as a life-long binding union between a man and a woman.

According to the book of Genesis, God created Adam first. (What did God say after He created Adam? "Hmmm…I think I can do better than that!") Then He created Eve and brought her to Adam and said, "For this reason a man will leave his father and mother and be united to his wife, and they will become one flesh" (Genesis 2:24). The phrase, "one flesh", which we will look at in greater detail later, indicates just how binding this union is in God's sight.

A COVENANT OF COMPANIONSHIP

Further, marriage is not just any type of covenant, but it is a covenant of companionship.[4] When God created man, He made him so that he would be lonely without an intimate companion with whom to live. In Genesis 2, after God created Adam, He said, "It is not good for the man to be alone. I will make a helper suitable for him" (verse 18). Adam knew the experience of being lonely.

How well do I recall the intense feelings of loneliness that swept over me after Beverley, a girl I dated for several months in high school, broke up with me. Friday evenings found me alone, instead of out on a date with her. It was about that same time that Bobby Vinton came out with his song, Mr. Lonely: "Lonely, I'm Mr. Lonely, /I have nobody for my own./ I'm so lonely, I'm Mr. Lonely,/ Wish I had someone to call on the phone."[5] I remember listening to that sad song on the radio, with tears streaming down my cheeks, identifying with Mr. Lonely. I wanted, more than anything, to be with Beverley. I was lonely.

After creating Adam and putting him in the garden, God had him name all the animals. "So the man gave names to all the livestock, the birds of the air and all the beasts of the field." But the scripture goes on to say,

"But for Adam, no suitable helper was found" (Genesis 2:20). So, to solve the problem of loneliness for Adam, God made a "helper suitable" for him. He made the woman and gave her to him for the "express purpose of solving the problem of his loneliness."[6]

> So the Lord God caused the man to fall into a deep sleep; and while he was sleeping, He took one of the man's ribs and closed up the place with flesh. Then the Lord God made a woman from the rib He had taken out of the man, and He brought her to the man. (Genesis 2:21–22)

Recently someone has claimed that a new discovery within the Dead Sea scrolls contains additional information as to how this actually took place. According to that story, Adam was walking around the Garden of Eden feeling very lonely. So God asked him, "What's the matter with you?" Adam said he was lonely and didn't have anyone to talk to. God said He was going to make Adam a companion and that it would be a woman.

He said, "This person will gather food for you, cook for you and when you discover clothing, she will wash it for you. She will always agree with every decision you make. She will bear your children and never ask you to get up in the middle of the night to take care of them. She will not nag you and will always be the first to admit she was wrong when you've had a disagreement. She will never have a headache and will freely give you love and passion whenever you want it."

Adam asked God, "What will a woman like this cost me?"

God replied, "An arm and a leg."

Then Adam asked, "What can I get for a rib?"

And the rest is history.[7]

Entrance into marriage means the desire to solve the other's need for companionship, and love in marriage focuses upon giving one's spouse what he/she needs to eliminate loneliness.

CONCLUSION

Three years after weeping as Bobby Vinton sang "Mr. Lonely", I was at a social event at Millar Memorial Bible Institute in Pambrun, Saskatchewan, where I had enrolled after high school. I looked across the room on that Friday evening, as the evening's social activities progressed. There I saw Linda. She was a classmate I had known for two years at Millar, but now, as I looked at her, all of a sudden I fell head over heels in love with her. She was, to my eyes, the most beautiful woman on the planet (Beverley didn't shine a candle beside her!) I could almost hear the song from the soundtrack of the musical, South Pacific, written by Rodgers and Hammerstein, "Some Enchanted Evening", in the background: "You may see a stranger, you may see a stranger, across a crowded room,/ and somehow you know, you know even then,/ that somewhere you'll see her, again and again."[8]

Two years later, I stood at the front of a church and

made a contract with her to be her husband until death parts us. And in the 35 years since, though we began on rocky ground, she and I have been great companions through this marvelous life God has given us. (That's a long time with one person, but it would have been a whole lot longer without her!) It's been a wonderful life.

I conclude this chapter with the lyrics of one of my son's favorite bands, U2, and their song, "A Man and a Woman":

> Little sister don't you worry about a thing today/ Take the heat from the sun/ Little sister I know that everything is not ok/ But you're like honey on my tongue/ True love never can be rent/ But only true love can keep beauty innocent/ I could never take a chance/ Of losing love to find romance/ In the mysterious distance/ Between a man and a woman/ No I could never take a chance/ 'Cause I could never understand/ The mysterious distance/ Between a man and a woman/ You can run from love/ And if it's really love it will find you/ Catch you by the heel/ But you can't be numb for love/ The only pain is to feel nothing at all/ How can I hurt when I'm holding you?/ I could never take a chance/ Of losing love to find romance/ In the mysterious distance/ Between a man and a woman/ And you're the one, there's no-one else/ who makes me want to lose myself/ In the mysterious distance/ Between a man and a woman/ Brown eyed girl across the street/ On rue Saint Divine/ I thought this is the one for me/ But she was already mine/ You were

already mine.../ Little sister/ I've been sleeping in the street again/ Like a stray dog/ Little sister I've been trying to feel complete again/ But you're gone and so is God/ The soul needs beauty for a soul mate/ When the soul wants...the soul waits.../ No I could never take a chance/ Of losing love to find romance/ In the mysterious distance/ Between a man and a woman/ For love and faith and sex and fear/ And all the things that keep us here/ In the mysterious distance/ Between a man and a woman/ How can I hurt when I'm holding you?[9]

QUESTIONS FOR SMALL GROUP DISCUSSION

1. Have you and your spouse ever had a funny experience like Henry did at the banquet he and Linda attended? Share it with your group.

2. What do you think of the Canadian government's new definition of marriage? Do you agree with it? Why or why not?

3. How legitimate is the argument that since God "invented" marriage, going to Him and His word is the best way for a married couple to live? Suggest some examples of God the inventor's guidelines for marriage from Scripture that you know will contribute to a good marriage.

4. Why would God expect marriage to be a life long relationship?

5. Do you agree that marriage is a contract between a man and a woman? What about people who don't get married and yet live together in a common-law relationship?

6. Had you ever heard of marriage described as a "covenant of companionship" before? What do you think of that concept?

7. Can you identify with Bobby Vinton's song "Mr. Lonely"? Have you ever been that lonely?

8. Can people be married and still be lonely? Why?

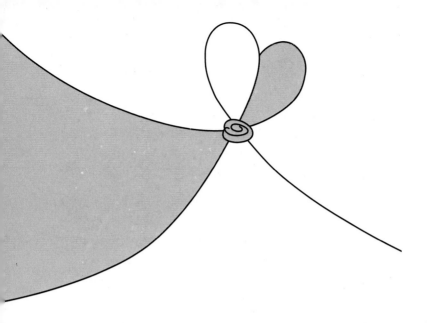

COME HELL OR HIGH-WATER

Over the years, I have performed wedding ceremonies for over a hundred couples. Some are more memorable than others. I will never forget one wedding ceremony, which I conducted just two weeks after breaking my collarbone. I was wearing what is called a "figure eight clavicle strap" to protect the broken bone. It was a hot day and still not fully recovered from the injury, part way through the service I found myself becoming uncertain on my feet. The bridesmaid was singing a song, which to me seemed interminable. As she got to the 13th verse, I decided to lean against the table behind me to rest a bit. I felt better, but shortly thereafter, I found myself becoming even hotter. Then, I smelled smoke. I glanced backwards over my shoulder and saw a column of smoke ascending to the ceiling of the church. I realized my jacket was on fire!

I had been leaning against the unity candle that sat on the table behind me. With my one good hand, I began to beat the flames out. I could see people in the congregation beginning to laugh (the bridesmaid, by now, was motoring on to verse 17). Fortunately, I succeeded in dousing the flames and somehow managed to finish the ceremony. After the ceremony was over, I went to my office to put away my books. One of the women in the church happened to be in the office. As I passed by her, she looked and saw the back of my jacket. I heard later that she went home and suggested to her husband that the church give me a raise. "Pastor Henry is wearing clothes with holes in them!" she reported to him. Unfortunately, he didn't heed her recommendation, and I am still awaiting that raise.

I, HENRY, DO TAKE YOU, LINDA

When a couple enters the covenant of marriage, they make promises to each other. These promises are called "vows." Each time I conduct a wedding ceremony, I ask the husband, "Will you give yourself to (and I name the girl) to be her husband; to love her, comfort her, honor and protect her; and forsaking all others, to be faithful to her so long as you both shall live?" And he responds to me, "I will!" (I then ask the same question of the girl.)

In those vows, they promise to be exclusively for the

other person until death parts them. No one else will ever be allowed to come between them. That promise is based on one of the Ten Commandments as found in Exodus 20:14: "You shall not commit adultery." Then, should they be tempted to be unfaithful, they will remember their promise to be faithful and follow through on their commitment. They make this commitment and, hopefully, plan to keep it no matter what.

I KEEP MY PROMISE

One Saturday morning, in a small village located in a valley next to a peaceful river, there was a sudden downpour that dumped several inches of rain on the area. Because of the heavy influx of water, the river rose rapidly and people living alongside the river had to evacuate their homes. Because it came so fast, some people only had time enough to climb onto the roofs of their houses and await rescue. Two women were sitting on the roof of a house when they noticed a baseball cap going up and down in the water beneath them.

"What in the world is *that?*" asked the one woman.

"Oh," said the other, "That's my husband Harry. He said he was going to mow the lawn this afternoon, come Hell or high-water."

The phrase, "Come Hell or high-water", has been used to describe a situation in which a person makes a commitment to do something and he/she is not going to let anything stop him/her from doing it. It is with that same mindset that we are to enter marriage. We are to be totally and completely committed to carrying out our contractual obligations.

Over the last few years, there have been a number of TV reality series: *Survivor, The Apprentice, Treasure Hunters, America's Next Top Model, The Mole, The Amazing Race, Big Brother,* just to name a few. One of those was called *Temptation Island.* In it, committed couples would allow themselves to be put into compromising situations and attempt to see how long each would remain committed to the other. Some resisted, some caved into the temptation.

In marriage, you may be tempted to be unfaithful, but because of the promises you have made to your spouse, you say to yourself, "No, I promised her; I promised him, I wouldn't do this." You may be playing around with a temptation right now; there may be someone other than your spouse to whom you find yourself growing more and more attracted to. You may be finding yourself becoming infatuated with them. It is in this time of attraction and infatuation that you remember your vows—what you said you would and would not do—and walk away from, not towards, that other person.

Satan will make the temptation so appealing that you will find yourself almost irresistibly drawn in that direction. I have heard people say, "It was as if I was drawn by a magnet." In these circumstances, it can be difficult to think rationally—but that is what you need to do. Here are some questions that you need to ask yourself when you are tempted to break your marriage vows and be unfaithful. They come from Randy Alcorn's article,

"Deterring Immorality by Counting Its Cost: The exorbitant price of sexual sin" in which he says:

> Whenever I feel particularly vulnerable to temptation, I find it helpful to review what effects my actions could have. Grieving the Lord who redeemed me, dragging His sacred name in the mud; one day having to look Jesus, the righteous judge, in the face and having to give an account of my actions; following in the footsteps of those people whose immorality forfeited their ministries and caused me to shudder; inflicting untold hurt on Nancy, my best friend and loyal wife; losing Nancy's respect and trust; hurting my beloved daughters Carina and Angie; destroying my example and credibility with my children and nullifying both present and future efforts to teach them to obey God (why listen to a man who betrayed Mom and us?); if blindness should continue, or my wife is unable to forgive, perhaps losing my wife and children forever; causing shame to my family; losing self respect; memories and flashbacks that could plague future intimacies with my wife; wasting years of ministry training and experience for a long time, maybe even permanently; forfeiting years of witnessing to my father and reinforcing his distrust for ministers that has begun to soften only recently by my example but that would harden perhaps permanently because of my immorality; undermining the faithful example and hard work of other Christians in our community (when you fall into sin it is not just you who are affected, all of us are too); bringing great pleasure to Satan, the enemy of God

and all that is good; heaping judgment and endless difficulty on the person with whom I committed adultery; possibly bearing the physical consequences of such diseases as Gonorrhea, Syphilis, Chlamydia, Herpes, and AIDS, perhaps infecting Nancy, and in the case of AIDS, perhaps causing her death; possibly causing pregnancy with all the personal and financial implications including a lifelong reminder of my sin; bringing hurt and shame to the pastors and elders that I know; causing hurt and shame to those I have led to Christ; invoking shame and lifelong embarrassment on myself. [10]

In the Bible, we read how Joseph, while serving as a steward in Potiphar's house in Egypt, experienced a tremendously strong temptation to be sexually immoral.

> So he left in Joseph's care everything he had; with Joseph in charge, he did not concern himself with anything except the food he ate. Now Joseph was well-built and handsome, and after a while his master's wife took notice of Joseph and said, "Come to bed with me!" But he refused. "With me in charge," he told her, "my master does not concern himself with anything in the house; everything he owns he has entrusted to my care. No one is greater in this house than I am. My master has withheld nothing from me except you, because you are his wife. How then could I do such a wicked thing and sin against God?" (Genesis 39:6–9)

Joseph had made a commitment to God to keep himself away from any compromises in his life. And, no matter how tempted, he remained faithful. That should be our commitment too.

DON'T BE A FOOL

We keep our marriage vows because God expects us to. One of the concerns I have when I lead couples through their wedding vows is that they go through them in a routine manner: I say it and they repeat it after me, while yawning (mentally). As a matter a fact, I must confess that even when I was getting married, I did so myself. Later, when Linda reminded me of the promises I had made to her, I remember responding, "I said *that?*" So, I tell them that I want them to ponder exactly what it is they are saying. I tell them it is important that they realize the seriousness of making a promise like that.

We keep our marriage vows because God expects us to keep them: "When you make a vow to God, do not delay in fulfilling it. He has no pleasure in fools; fulfill your vow. It is better not to vow than to make a vow and not fulfill it. Do not let your mouth lead you into sin" (Ecclesiastes 5:4–6). Marriage is a commitment where, at the altar, you both determine, "I am in this for the rest of my life!" Linda and I have had our fair share of struggles, particularly in the early years of marriage. But we were always committed to each other. We believe divorce is not an option.

Over the years, I have observed a number of

Christian marriages breaking up, and this has always distressed me as a pastor. The key issue behind some of those breakups has been the fact that people have broken their promises; they have said, "I will" and later, they didn't!

You have husbands who said they would love their wives like Christ loved the church and then, in the years following, have not. I am reminded of the cartoon I once saw in which a disgruntled wife is saying to her husband, "You promised to be humbly grateful but you turned out to be grumbly hateful!"

You also have wives who promised to honor and respect their husbands, and they have not. This was the case in which a couple went to the marriage counselor and the husband shared how frustrated he was with his wife.

"When we were first married," he told the counselor, "whenever I came home from work, I would be met by her bringing me my slippers and by the dog barking. Now, when I come home, the dog brings my slippers and she barks."

"What are you complaining about?" asked the counselor. "You're still getting the same service!"

But as result of these failures to keep their commitments, hurts come in and unforgiveness settles in. And so, against their word that they gave 5, 10, and 15 or more years ago, in which they said they would not leave the marriage, they do.

A PERSON OF INTEGRITY

Why is keeping your marriage vows so serious? It is so crucial because it reveals one's true character. The most important aspect of our personhood is that of our character. And the key part of character is our integrity—whether or not we keep our word. James 5:12 instructs us, "Let your 'Yes' be yes, and your 'No,' no, or you will be condemned."

The word "integrity" is from the root word "integer" meaning "one." From that, we get "integrated" which means "to be whole" or "to be complete." If you have no integrity, it shows that your character is rotten to the core. An example of a person with little integrity, in my opinion, is former American president, Bill Clinton. Clinton who, while he was having an affair with White House intern Monica Lewinski, insisted, with his finger wagging, "I did not have sexual relations with that woman!" Yet, all the while, he *was* engaging in sex with her.

IN GOOD TIMES AND BAD

We keep our promises even when it is not easy to. One set of vows I have used in marrying couples has the husband saying to the wife, "I give to you, in the presence of God and these witnesses, my pledge to stay by your side as your faithful husband, *in sickness and in health, in joy and in sorrow, as well as through the good times and the bad.*"

The "health", "joy" and "good times" is the easy part; the tough part is the "sickness", "sorrow" and "bad times."

I heard about a woman who went to a judge and said, "I want a divorce."

He asked, "Why?"

She replied, "I don't like him."

The judge responded, "But you promised to take him for better or worse."

"Yeah," she shot back, "but he's a lot worse than I took him for."

Chuck Swindoll, in a message on marital commitment, asks the rhetorical question: "What does *'for worse'* mean?"[11] Many people only see the option of "for better" as the basis for fulfilling their marriage vows.

If I tell you I am going to do something, integrity in my character means that I follow through and do it, even if it is painful for me. In Psalm 15:1, David asks, "LORD, who may dwell in your sanctuary? Who may live on your holy hill?" Then, among a list of other things, includes, "He who...keeps his oath even when it hurts" (Verse 4).

My mom and dad were married 67 years until cancer took my mother's life at the age of 89. During the months of her illness, I watched my father as he stood by mom's side, taking care of her, making meals (something he had never done before), and loving her. I remember watching him and thinking, *Now, that's keeping your marriage vows...*

In a recent edition of Leadership magazine,

Robertson McQuilkin tells how his wife was diagnosed with the dreaded Alzheimer's disease. As the disease progressed, McQuilkin had to make a serious decision: either put his wife into institutional care or quit his position as president of a large college and seminary and take care of her himself. He tells how he came to the decision to resign and take care of her:

> When the time came, the decision was firm. It took no great calculation. It was a matter of integrity. Had I not promised, forty-two years before: 'in sickness and in health...till death do us part?' As a man of my word, integrity has something to do with it. This was no grim duty to which I stoically resigned, however. It was only fair. She had, after all, cared for me for almost four decades with marvelous devotion; now it was my turn. And such a partner she was! If I took care of her for forty years, I would never be out of her debt.
>
> There is more: I love Muriel. She is a delight to me—her childlike dependence and confidence in me, her warm love, flashes of that wit I used to relish so, her happy spirit and tough resilience in the face of her distressing frustration. I do not have to care for her. I get to! But how could I walk away from a ministry God had so blessed during our twenty-two years at Columbia Bible College and Seminary? Not easily. So many dreams were yet on the drawing board. And the peerless team God had brought together—not just professionals but dear friends—how could I bear to leave them? But whatever Columbia needed,

it did not need a part-time, distracted leader. It was better to move out and let God designate a leader to step in while the momentum was continuing. It seemed clearly in the best interest of the ministry for me to step down, even if board and administrators thought otherwise. Both loves—for Muriel and for Columbia Bible College and Seminary—dictated the same choice. I have been startled by the response to the announcement of my resignation. Husbands and wives renew their marriage vows, pastors tell the story to their congregations. It was a mystery to me, until a distinguished oncologist, who lives constantly with dying people, told me, "Almost all women stand by their men; very few men stand by their women." It is more than keeping promises and being fair, however. As I watch her brave descent into oblivion, Muriel is the joy of my life. Daily I discern new manifestations of the kind of person she is, the wife I always loved. I also see fresh manifestations of God's love–the God I long to love more fully.[12]

That is what I am talking about. May it be for you as one couple who, married for many years, put it to me, "We married for keeps."

QUESTIONS FOR SMALL GROUP DISCUSSION

1. Have you ever been to a wedding where something especially funny happened? Share that experience with your group.

2. Do you remember your wedding vows? Do you ever think about them as it concerns your marriage relationship? How important is keeping those vows to you?

3. How important is your own integrity? On a scale of 1–10, with 10 being the highest, how would you rate yourself at keeping your word and the promises that you have made?

4. Do you agree with the statement that "keeping your marriage vows is so crucial because it reveals one's true character"? Why or why not?

5. Discuss Joseph's temptation to become sexually involved with Potiphar's wife according to Genesis 39:6–9. How did he handle it? What lessons can you draw for yourself from his experience?

6. Why does God look so negatively at people who do not keep their vows? What is so bad about breaking your vows? Why is keeping your word so important in His eyes?

7. Why do people find the "sickness", "sorrow" and "bad times" part of their vows so difficult to keep?

Answer Chuck Swindoll's rhetorical question, "What does 'for worse' mean?"

8. Did the story of Robertson McQuilkin's decision to resign from his position of college and seminary president to take care of his Alzheimer's stricken wife make an impact on you? What was it? How did it affect you?

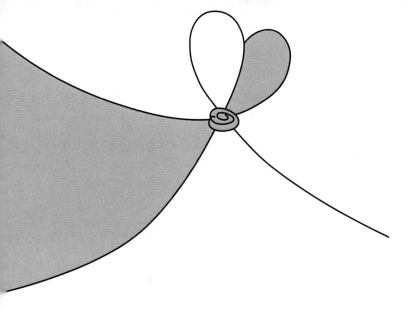

HOW TO BE HAPPY THOUGH MARRIED

A dietician was addressing a large audience in Chicago. "The material we put into our stomachs is enough to have killed most of us sitting here years ago," she began. "Red meat is awful. Soft drinks erode our stomach's lining. Chinese food is loaded with MSG. Vegetables can be disastrous and none of us realizes the long term harm caused by the germs in our drinking water.

"But," she went on to say, "There is one thing that is the most dangerous of all and we all have, or will, eat it. Can anyone tell me what food it is that causes the most grief and suffering for years after eating it?" An elderly man sitting in the front row stood up and said, "Wedding cake."

I am sure that everyone who gets married does so with the confident expectation that they will be happy in that new relationship. No one starts out on their wedding day by saying, "We're going to have marriage problems, we're going to separate and divorce." All are starry-eyed about their prospects of riding off into the sunset and living happily ever after.

Unfortunately however, in many cases, people are unhappy though married. A recent survey that I came across stated that a staggering 60% of those who are marrying today will break up. They went on to say that even for those who stay married, relationships between women and men are becoming more difficult, fragile, and unhappy.

A young couple was getting married and the groom was exceptionally nervous. Uncertain as to the next step in the marriage ceremony, he whispered to the minister, "Is it kisstomary to cuss the bride?" The minister responded, "Not now. Later." Sadly that is too true. J. Paul Getty, who was one of the first people in the world to amass a fortune of over $1 billion U.S. dollars, said, "I hate to be a failure. I hate and regret the failure of my marriages. I would gladly give all my millions for just one lasting marital success."[13]

I believe that the key to being happy though married is to understand and apply God's prescriptions for marriage as laid down in the scriptures. Part of the understanding we need comes from the Bible's teaching on roles in marriage, roles that God has ordained for men and for women.

MAN THE INITIATOR

The Book of Genesis in the Bible informs us that God created Adam first. "The Lord God formed the man from the dust of the ground and breathed into his nostrils the breath of life, and the man became a living being" (Genesis 2:7). Following that, He created Eve: "So the Lord God caused the man to fall into a deep sleep; and while he was sleeping, he took one of the man's ribs and closed up the place with flesh. Then the Lord God made a woman from the rib he had taken out of the man, and he brought her to the man" (Genesis 2:21–22). It is interesting to note that Dr. James Young Simpson, on November 8, 1847, got the idea for his invention of anesthesia from reading this passage.

Someone has said that the advantage both Adam and Eve had in their marriage relationship from being created in this manner was that he didn't have to hear about all the men she could have married and she didn't have to hear about the way his mother cooked! But when He created man and woman, God created the husband to be the initiator and the wife to be the responder. This can be seen from the original Hebrew words used in the text. The Hebrew word of "male" is "piercer" and for "female" is "pierced." There are the obvious sexual implications to that as well, but God was establishing a pattern He wanted followed in marriage: man as the initiator and woman as the responder.

The Bible uses a particular term when it describes the husband's role as initiator. It is the word "head."

"For the husband is the head of the wife as Christ is the head of the church, his body, of which he is the Savior" (Ephesians 5:23). Notice it does not say the husband is to "be" the head, it says he "is." God sees the husband as the head.

JOB DESCRIPTION FOR HEADS

What does God mean, when He says the husband is the head? Does it mean he is the dictator in the family, the only one with a say, the tyrant who rules from his invincible castle? The answer: No! If a husband dominates his wife like a dictator would a country, it is evident that he is not carrying out the Bible's expectations, as we will soon see. It disturbs me that some men take the teaching on headship in the Bible as basis for male superiority. Out of that often comes the abuse of women, even sexual abuse, and it is this teaching that has been used to justify it. This is a total misrepresentation of the teaching of headship in the Bible!

When God says the husband is the head, it means he assumes responsibility to provide spiritual leadership for the home and to establish its direction. Some time ago, Linda and I were at a marriage seminar, and each of us had to do an assignment. We were to ask each other for our number one request. I was surprised when her request of me was: "Take the spiritual leadership in the home." When I asked her how she wanted me to fulfill that, she gave me three points: 1. Grow yourself, 2. Encourage me, 3. Teach our children.

THE PROBLEM OF MALE PASSIVITY

Unfortunately, many men do not carry out this role of leadership in their marriage. Why not? I have observed there are at least three reasons for this. First, some men are paralyzed by the fear of failure. As result, they do not take the initiative. It is easier to not attempt than to try and fail. Failure is so painful.

Secondly, there are others for whom the greater priority is meeting their own significance needs through their work and career. The family and the home are put on the back burner.

This was what I was doing in the early years of our marriage. After we got married, I became obsessed with becoming a success in ministry. Our church was a brand new church that desperately needed to grow in order to survive. To make that happen, I worked long, long hours. In our first year of married life together, I later counted and found that I had spent only six evenings at home, alone with Linda. Most of the rest of the time, I was gone, working at the church. My goal was to have a large, vibrant church that pointed to my successful work as a pastor. But in the meantime, she was literally dying on the vine. She felt completely neglected and ignored, even abandoned by me.

Then in the fall of 1980, after seven years of this kind of marriage, I took a course in counseling at the seminary I was enrolled in as a part-time student, while completing my Master's degree. The teacher was Dr. Larry Crabb, and that class had an absolutely amazing and freeing effect on me. I realized for the first time in my life why I was so driven to succeed: I was depending on the success of the church to make me feel like a worthwhile person. I had believed that my entire sense of worth as a man came from being a success in the ministry.

It was the truth that my worth as a man came, not from my success in ministry (which is so fraught with uncertainty anyway), but rather from the fact that I was a child of God that set me free. Because God loves and accepts me, I am secure. Because I am in Christ, I am significant.

As result, I began to see myself as already worthwhile in Christ and the drivenness that had characterized my earlier life totally vanished. I was set free from my obsession to succeed in ministry and could finally become the husband Linda needed and the father my growing family required. The change was immediate and gratifying to Linda.

I have asked Linda to describe that change and here is how she saw it: "Henry was quite impressed with the truths he was learning at this course and we spent hours listening to the tapes of the lectures. He preached on the topic and talked to everyone about what he was learning. I was skeptical–wondering if what he said he had learned was actually going to become a reality in his life. He began changing–wanting to be more involved in the family and wanting to spend more time with me. I waited...and the change remained! He had become a different husband and a different father."

My marriage was saved because of this truth I had learned. As you can see, that happened over twenty-six years ago, and it is still as true to me today as it was back when I first learned it.

MAN THE MOUNTAIN-CLIMBER

Third, many men are passive because they live their lives by conquering challenges. I refer to this phenomenon as "man the mountain-climber." For them, there is always a new challenge to overcome. Dating is the initial challenge—capturing the highly desired prize, the pretty girl. But the thrill of that capture soon wears off. They then begin to look for a new mountain to climb and conquer, be it a career, becoming independently wealthy, starting a new business or even another woman. But they are constantly looking for new challenges.

One of the ways I have personally overcome the tendency towards passivity in my marriage relationship has been to set a new goal to conquer. That new goal for me is, every day, to try to please Linda and keep her happy, to the best of my ability. I tell husbands, tongue in cheek, that when you set that as your new goal, you can rest assured you will never reach it. You will never get to the top of that mountain! Each new day, you start all over again, in pleasing her and keeping her happy.

THE PROBLEM OF FEMALE FEAR

Now the discussion of a husband's leadership can also

promote feelings of fear amongst some women. Why? For some women, it may come from bad experiences they have had with men previously: men who've used them, abused them, and hurt them. Any mention of leadership sounds a lot like the abuse and trampling they have previously experienced.

On the other hand, it may come from a fear that their husband may not fully meet their needs. So to follow a husband's leadership means a loss of control to them. To commit themselves to their husband's leadership would put them in a very vulnerable situation that they would rather stay away from.

HUSBANDS, LOVE YOUR WIVES

The Bible's solution to this fear for women is for husbands to provide this leadership in a loving manner. "Husbands, love your wives and do not be harsh with them" (Colossians 3:19). The Message translates it this way: "Husbands, go all out in love for your wives. Don't take advantage of them."

Ephesians 5 lists three ways a husband shows love to his wife. First, he is to love his wife as Christ loved the church. "Husbands, love your wives, just as Christ loved the church and gave himself up for her" (Ephesians 5:25). When Howard Hendricks was professor at Dallas Theological Seminary, one of his students came to see him.

"Prof, I have a problem," he said, "I love my wife too much."

Hendricks says he blinked and said, "Run that by me again. I hear it so seldom."

He then took the young man to this passage and asked him, "Do you love her that much?" "Oh no, of course not!" he replied.

Hendricks concludes, "I said to him, 'Then get with it!'"[14]

Someone has said, "If you think it's possible you love your wife too much, you probably haven't loved her enough." A husband sacrificially lays down his life for her; he loses himself for her. Even when it is difficult, he still does it.

Secondly, he is to love his wife as his own body. "In this same way, husbands ought to love their wives as their own bodies. He who loves his wife loves himself. After all, no one ever hated his own body, but he feeds and cares for it, just as Christ does the church" (Ephesians 5:28–29). A husband tenderly takes care of his wife just as he does his body. Most guys care for their bodies. I know; over the years, I've watched a lot of them eat.

The deepest need of a woman is to feel cherished. The word that is translated as "cares for" is "thalpo" and it means "to cherish with tender love, to foster with tender care." Because I am relationally challenged, I found I had to ask Linda what being cherished meant to her. Her answer was to give me an illustration of a time when I had fostered her with tender care. It was when she had had her cancer surgery. After the operation, I had to take care of her completely, as she was unable to do anything for herself. When I brought her home from the hospital, I helped her walk from the hospital to the car and then from the car to the house. I took care of the children, made the meals, cleaned the house, and made sure she was comfortable. "That is when I really felt cherished!" she said to me. A man cherishes his wife when her welfare is more important to him than anything else.

Third, he is to love his wife as he already loves himself. It is very natural for every man to love himself. So he simply begins to love her like he already loves himself. That self love is best encapsulated in a little ditty I memorized long ago: "I love me, I think I'm grand./ I go to the movies, I hold my hand./ I put my arm around my waist,/ and when I get fresh, I slap my face!"

Some have challenged me about my statement that all men do love themselves. "What about people who hate themselves, even to the point of killing themselves?" they ask. My response is that people who say they hate themselves and even go as far as to hurt themselves still really do love themselves. This reaction of self-hatred stems from such a disappointment with their original love for themselves that, in their disillusionment, they do go as far as to hurt themselves. But at the core of their being is still an incredible sense of love for themselves driving it all.

When a husband loves his wife in these three ways as laid out in scripture, he will provide his wife with all she needs to feel secure in his love. Indeed, my observation over the years has been this: I doubt if there is a woman who would have a difficult time submitting to a man who loves her to the point he would die for her.

A number of years ago, at the Billy Graham School of Evangelism, I heard Ron Blanc tell of an occasion when he went to listen to the radical feminist, Gloria Steinem, speak. At a break, he went up to the front and asked her,

"Were you ever married?"

"Yes," she responded.

"Was it a happy experience?" he further asked.

"No," was her reply.

He went on to say to her, "You said tonight that Christianity puts women down. It doesn't. It tells a man he is to love his wife."

Then he read the passage on love from 1 Corinthians 13: 4–7 to her.

> Love is very patient and kind, never jealous or envious, never boastful or proud, never haughty or selfish or rude. Love does not demand its own way. It is not irritable or touchy. It does not hold grudges and will hardly even notice when others do it wrong. It is never glad about injustice, but rejoices whenever truth wins out. If you love someone, you will be loyal to him no matter what the cost. You will always believe in him, always expect the best of him, and always stand your ground in defending him. (TLB)

"This is how a man is to love his wife," he said to her.

Do you know what Gloria Steinem's response to

him was? Quite vehemently, she stated, "There is no such man!"

Well, there need to be "such men," and I challenge you guys reading this to become such a man.

WOMAN THE RESPONDER

As God created the man to be the initiator, so He also created the woman to be the responder. In the ideal marriage, when the man initiates as God would have him to, the woman will respond positively, automatically. In many ways, she is like a flower. If a flower receives sunshine, rain and fertilizer, it opens up in all its glory. This was the case with the Beloved in King Solomon's life. She says:

> Like an apple tree among the trees of the forest is my lover among the young men. I delight to sit in his shade, and his fruit is sweet to my taste. He has taken me to the banquet hall, and his banner over me is love. Strengthen me with raisins, refresh me with apples, for I am faint with love.
>
> Song of Solomon 2:3–5

But, if on the other hand, the sun and rain and fertilizer are withheld, the flower dries up and its glory is not seen. Many a woman is literally dying because her husband is not initiating as God would have him to.

As I said before, I doubt if there is a woman who would have a difficult time responding positively to a man who loves her like he already loves himself, like he loves his own body, and like Christ loves the church. However, when the husband falls down in how he initiates, it makes it much more difficult for the wife. If that loving initiation is not forthcoming, there is hurt and as a consequence, over a period of time, she begins to close her spirit to him. One woman told me of the hurt experienced in her first week of marriage when her new husband put his son from his first marriage ahead of her that very first weekend. Another woman shared with me that she watched as her husband, who had courted her and won her heart before marriage, began to systematically neglect her and her needs after marriage. When I asked her how that had made her feel, with great intensity in her voice she replied, "I felt so trapped! I felt betrayed!"

As a result, what happens next is most interesting. After being so let down by what the husband has failed to initiate, many women commit what I call "emotional divorce." They begin to pull away from their husband and distance themselves emotionally from him to protect themselves from further hurt. Many build walls around themselves that, even if, later, he should try, he cannot get through. Sometimes, that eventually leads to a physical divorce.

WOMAN THE FORGIVER

Now, no man is perfect and, if you live together long enough, every woman will have her fair share of hurts.

A woman's greatest temptation will be to get angry and then bitter at her husband for his failure to love her as she desires. That is why she must learn, even more, to be a forgiver. That is why Jesus said, "And when you stand praying, if you hold anything against anyone, forgive him, so that your Father in heaven may forgive you your sins" (Mark 11:25).

One woman told me that when her husband left her for another woman following many years of marriage, she developed an unforgiving spirit against him. "Then," she told me, "last winter one morning, God woke me up and said, 'Forgive him!'" She went on to say, "I did and I felt like I was wrapped in a warm blanket."

In a God-honoring marriage, the wife remains responsive and loving toward her husband through forgiveness. At the same time, the sensitive husband sees to it that he provides for his wife's needs so that she can respond positively and become the woman God intended for her to be all along.

Unfortunately, we must recognize the reality that there will be some men who simply will not provide for their wife's needs, no matter what she does. What do you do, as a godly wife, in such a case? First, affirm the truth in your life that, in Christ, you are already secure and worthwhile as a person. Even if your husband is not there for you, God is. In His sight, you are a worthwhile and valuable person. "I will give thanks to You, for I am fearfully and wonderfully made; Wonderful are Your works, and my soul knows it very well" (Psalm 139:14, NASB-U). If that core need of worthwhileness is fully met in the One who created you, you can carry on, even in a loveless relationship, because your sense of security comes from Him, not him. I admit that it would be a lot nicer and easier if your husband fully met your needs. But if he does not, be assured that God is enough. As Corrie ten Boom who, together with her sister, Betsy, suffered in a Nazi concentration camp during World War II, put it, "There is no pit so deep that God's love is not deeper still."[15] May that be your experience too.

WHAT GOD WANTS FROM A WIFE

There are also things the scriptures teach the wife she needs to do. There are two ways she needs to respond to her husband. First, she is to respect him. "However, each one of you also must love his wife as he loves himself, and the wife must respect her husband" (Ephesians 5:33). In the ideal, Biblical marriage, a husband initiates loving leadership and the wife responds respectfully.

She shows that respect by holding him in high esteem. A number of years ago, I was at a conference where a missionary and his wife were called to the front to present their work. I will never forget watching as the husband made his presentation and his wife stood at his side. What made the impact on me was to see how she was looking at him as he spoke. Her eyes were filled with admiration as she looked at him, and I recall how it stirred me very deeply. I remember a desire to be similarly admired by my wife arising within me as I watched her admiring him.

A wife shows respect by regarding what he says and does as valuable and verbally expressing to him her admiration of him. I once sat in my office with a couple going through major marital conflict. One of the issues was the fact that he was inept in a number of areas, and she was becoming more and more frustrated with and by him. Again, I will never forget the venom with which she spat out at her husband: "He's such a dummy!" He simply dropped his head as she said it. Even if he was less than adequate in her estimation, she was still required by God to respect him.

The second area which the scriptures teach a wife how to respond to her husband is by (I say this cautiously) submitting to his leadership. "Wives, submit to your husbands as to the Lord. For the husband is the head of the wife as Christ is the head of the church, his body, of which he is the Savior. Now as the church submits to Christ, so also wives should submit to their husbands in everything" (Ephesians 5:22–24).

I recognize that when I, as a man, write to women on this topic, there is the potential for misunderstanding and hurt feelings. Some pastors seek to avoid that by not addressing this issue at all. They may be like the fellow that I heard at a Gaither concert I recently attended. He was sharing why he and his wife were still so happy after so many years of marriage. He said, "I have discovered that I can choose to be right or I can choose to be happy. I choose to be happy!" Comedian Jeff Allen says, "Happy wife, happy life!" However, I choose to teach God's word, and as I write on the topic of women's submission to their husbands, I do so with the utmost of respect and honor for women.

The common image that the concept "submission" raises is of a floor mat. It suggests that the husband is the dictator in the home who can do whatever he pleases. He yells "Jump!" and on the way up, she asks, "How high?" As I have already stated, that position has been used to justify all sorts of abuse by men to their wives. I have said that that view is completely in error. But what does the Bible mean when it talks about submission?

HIERARCHISM IN THE UNIVERSE

The Greek word for "submit" is *hupotasso,* and it means "to arrange your life under." As I see it, hierarchism (submission to those in authority over us) is built into the warp and woof of the universe. For example, when Jesus was approached by the centurion in Capernaum to heal his servant, Jesus said He would go and do it. But the centurion replied,

> Lord, I do not deserve to have you come under my roof. But just say the word, and my servant will be healed. For I myself am a man under authority, with soldiers under me. I tell this one, Go, and he goes; and that one, Come, and he comes. I say to my servant, Do this, and he does it.
>
> Matthew 8:8–9

This centurion recognized that the universe operates on the principle of a chain of command, as established by God Himself. He appealed to that principle in this case: for Jesus to simply use His authority to command the healing of His servant. We go on to read: "When Jesus heard this, he was astonished and said to those following him, 'I tell you the truth, I have not found anyone in Israel with such great faith'" (Matthew 8:10).

Even Jesus Himself lived with this hierarchical understanding. He was submissive to the authority of His Heavenly Father: "For I have come down from heaven not to do my will but to do the will of him who sent me" (John 6:38). He also prayed, "Father, if you are willing, take this cup from me; yet not my will, but yours be done" (Luke 22:42).

Husbands themselves have an authority that they themselves are to submit to. That authority is none other than Jesus Christ. "Now I want you to realize that the head of every man is Christ, and the head of the woman is man, and the head of Christ is God" (I Corinthians 11:3). Husbands are part of that same hierarchy themselves.

In regards to submission, wives are told to submit to their husbands "as to the Lord" (Ephesians 5:22). A wife's submission to her husband is as an act of submission to the Lord, first of all. That means accepting this divine pattern as being the original design of the Creator. This does not imply inequality; sameness is not necessary for equality. Furthermore, roles do not imply inferiority! Submission in marriage is accomplished when a wife recognizes and accepts her husband's leadership. It does not mean not being allowed to give your opinion or even have one.

To me, headship means that I seek out my wife's opinion and take it into consideration. Indeed, if I found Linda didn't want to do something, I would seriously reconsider my own intention. I would ask myself, "Where have I been insensitive to her?" In a good strong Christian marriage, the husband will never abuse his God-given authority. When a man loves his wife as Christ loved the church, he will never knowingly do anything to hurt her. In our marriage, I would never force Linda to do anything. I never yell at her to submit or even suggest that she should. To me, her resistance is always a signal that something may be wrong on my part as spiritual leader: either I am not fully aware of the situation or I am not concerned enough, not loving enough, not gentle enough. I realize, something is wrong.

TRUST IS NEEDED

Further, the wife will trust her husband to not intentionally hurt her.

> For this is the way the holy women of the past who put their hope in God used to make themselves beautiful. They were submissive to their own husbands, like Sarah, who obeyed Abraham and called him her master. You are her daughters if you do what is right and do not give way to fear.
>
> 1 Peter 3:5–6

One of the basic building blocks of a strong marriage is trust. Nothing destroys a marriage sooner than suspicion. Now I recognize that the danger of trust is that you can be betrayed, and betrayal is painful. Suspicion helps you "prepare" for that. But it never builds a marriage. I would rather go for it and trust and have the possibility of a good marriage than not to trust and guarantee a terrible marriage.

In that same passage, Peter instructs the husbands: "Husbands, in the same way be considerate as you live with your wives, and treat them with respect as the weaker partner and as heirs with you of the gracious gift of life, so that nothing will hinder your prayers" (1 Peter 3:7). Notice the phrase, "hinder your prayers." How crucial it is that I, as a husband, be sensitive to my wife's needs because if I am not, my prayers will not be answered by God! How important is that?

A wife submits to her husband as the church submits to Christ. The marriage relationship on earth is a picture of God's relationship with us; the believer's union with Christ is a model of how a wife relates to her husband. So, when a husband loves his wife and a wife respects her husband, it shows on earth what the relationship between Jesus and the church is like in Heaven.

QUESTIONS FOR SMALL GROUP DISCUSSION

1. Everyone has heard some good marriage jokes. Share one with your group as you begin this session. (Then send a copy of it to Dr. Henry A. Ozirney, Box 22, Stonewall, Mb. ROC 2ZO Canada.)

2. What is your opinion of the Bible's teaching on the roles God has ordained for husbands and wives? Do you agree with His wisdom in setting marriage up to function in that manner? Why or why not?

3. Discuss the concept of the husband being the "head" of the wife. How do you see that headship being carried out appropriately? What are some abuses of it that you have observed in other marriages?

4. Why are many husbands passive when it comes to their marriage relationship? What factors in their lives contribute to that?

5. Discuss the three ways men are told to love their wives. How would that actually look in a marriage?

6. Discuss the concept of the wife being the responder to the husband's initiation? What makes it difficult for wives to react positively?

7. Discuss the concept of a wife's submission to her husband. Why do many women react negatively to this idea?

8. Why is emotional divorce such a great temptation for many wives? How and why would you counsel a woman to learn to be a forgiver?

9. What would you say to a woman whose husband makes no attempt to love his wife as Christ loved the church? How should she respond?

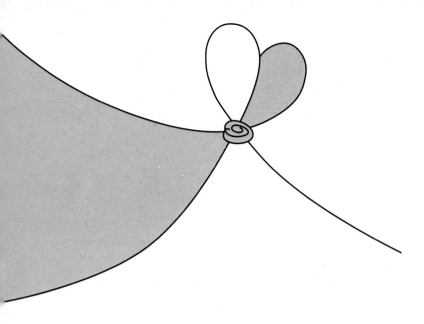

WHAT IS LOVE?

When our two oldest boys were young, nine and six, they went through what I called the "girl-hating" stage. If I said the word "love," they were ready to die. To them, there was nothing worse than having to kiss a girl. Whenever I kissed Linda, they would cover their eyes and ask, "Is it over?" They simply could not fathom how anyone could want to have anything to do with anyone of the opposite sex. When I asked them why they felt that way, they told me that you could get the "cooties" from girls. Well, they are long past that stage now. Our oldest son is happily married and has two sons of his own.

But kids do have some funny ideas about love. Recently, someone e-mailed me some "Tips on Love" as given by young children. For example, when asked for their opinions on love, Anita, age six, said, "I'm in favor of love as long as it doesn't happen when the Simpson's are on TV." Bobby, six, responded, "Love will find you even if you are trying to hide from it. I have been trying to hide from it since I've been five, but the girls keep finding me." Regina, 10, offered: "I'm not rushing into love. I'm finding fourth grade hard enough."

When asked why love happens between two particular people, Jan, age nine, said, "No one is sure why it happens, but I heard it has something to do with how you smell. That's why perfume and deodorant are so popular." Harlan, eight, suggested, "I think you're supposed to get shot with an arrow or something, but the rest isn't supposed to be so painful."

In the English language, the word "love" is used in many different ways. You can say, "I love my wife", or "I love donuts." The difference, however, between the two can be quite substantial; I think you will agree. Thus, the concept of love can be quite confusing so let's see if we can straighten out some of that confusion.

THE WORLD'S VIEW OF LOVE

After I graduated from high school, I enrolled at Millar Memorial Bible Institute and in my first year there, I must confess, I did not have any particular interest in a girl by the name of Linda Fordyce. Indeed, for the first two years, I rarely paid any attention to her. But when I went back for my third year, everything changed. In one evening, I fell head over heels in love with her.

In the weeks and months that followed, I was on Cloud Nine. My heart would do handsprings whenever I saw her. While at college, I learned a song that pretty well described what I was like in those days: "I walked up the door and I opened up the stairs,/ I said my pajamas and I put on my prayers,/ I turned off the bed and I jumped into the light./ All because she kissed me good night!"

Was it ever a good feeling!

LOVE IS A FEELING

Many people assume that love is a feeling you get. Like the little boy's definition of love: "Love is a feeling you feel, like you never felt before." But is love a feeling? Many people believe it is. I remember hearing of a fellow who left his wife for some young thing. When asked why he did it, he responded: "For the first time in my life, I feel love!" But is that love?

James Dobson describes it this way:

> The confusion begins when boy meets girl and the entire sky lights up in romantic profusion. Smoke and fire are followed by lightning and thunder, and alas, two trembly-voiced adolescents find themselves knee deep in true love. Adrenalin and 64 other hormones are dumped into the cardiovascular system by the pint and every nerve is charged with 110 volts

of electricity. Then two little fellows go racing up the respective backbones and blast their exhilarating message into each spinning head: "This is it! You've found the perfect human being! Hooray for love!"[16]

But unfortunately that is not love, it is really infatuation. Now infatuation is neither good nor bad, it just is. Everyone gets a good feeling when someone of the opposite sex is very fond of them. But the danger is to fall in love with a feeling and to assume that the feeling is love. That is dangerous because that feeling eventually and inevitably leaves. Like Gordon Lightfoot's song "If You Could Read My Mind" says, "The feeling's gone and I just can't get it back, I don't know where we went wrong."[17]

In his book, *The Five Love Languages,* Gary Chapman says research shows that the feelings of infatuation have about a two year "shelf life."[18] Recently I came across some research by Italian scientists that suggests romantic feelings of love lasts little more than a year. Working at the University of Pavia, these scientists claim to have found a brain chemical which was likely to be responsible for the first flush of love. Researchers said "raised levels of a protein were linked to feelings of euphoria and dependence experienced at the start of a relationship. But after studying people in long and short term relationships as well as single people, they found those levels receded in time."[19]

Writing in the Psychoneuroendocrinology Journal, the scientists reported, "The team analyzed alterations in proteins known as neurotrophins in the bloodstreams of men and women aged 18 to 31. They looked at 58 people who had recently started a relationship and compared the protein levels in the same number of people in long-term relationships and single people. In those who had just started a relationship, levels of a protein called Nerve Growth Factors, which causes tell-tale signs such as sweaty palms and the butterflies, were significantly higher. Of the 39 people who were still in the same new relationship after a year, the levels of NGF had been reduced to normal levels."

"Report co-author Piergluigi Politi said the findings did not mean people were no longer in love, just that it was not such an 'acute love.' He went on to say, 'The love became more stable. Romantic love seemed to have ended.' And he added the report suggested the change in love was due to a drop in NGF. 'Our current knowledge of the neurobiology of romantic love remains scanty. But it seems from this study, biochemical mechanisms could be involved in the mood changes that occur from the early stage of love to when the relationship becomes more established.' However, he said further research was needed.

"Dr. Lance Workman, head of psychology at Bath Spa University, said: 'Research has suggested that romantic love fades after a few years and becomes companionate love and it seems certain biological factors play a role'."[20]

Conventional wisdom tells us that when this feeling leaves, we should also leave the marriage relationship we are in. But my point is that that feeling is not love, but simply infatuation. Let me also say this: it is easy to become infatuated with someone else while married to your spouse. Infatuation is simply a feeling that leaves, sooner than later. I tell people to never act on an infatuation, *especially* if you are already married. Instead, pray and ask God to take the infatuation away, and He will. I have a number of testimonies to that effect.

Now if love *were* a feeling, it would be impossible to obey many of Christ's commands, such as: "love your enemies." How can you love someone you have no feelings for, someone who is out to get you? If love were just a feeling, it would be impossible.

R.C. Sproul tells the story about a man who visited his minister for counsel about his failing marriage. He told him that since love had exited the marriage, he was considering a divorce.

He looked to the pastor for any small portent of hope that the marriage might still be salvaged. The pastor gave his advice in simple terms.

"Sir, the Bible says that husbands must love their wives. Therefore, it is your Christian duty to go home and start loving your wife."

The man was incredulous.

"How can I do that? That is precisely the problem. That's why I came to you in the first place. The fact is, I don't love my wife anymore. That's why I want out. Can't you give me any better advice?"

The pastor was undeterred by the man's rejection of

his counsel and took a different tact. He suggested an alternate plan:

"Why don't you try a trial separation? Try moving next door for a few weeks and see if that helps."

The man was growing impatient and shot back,

"What good will that do? How can living next door help?"

The pastor replied,

"Doesn't God command us to love our neighbors? Maybe if you lived as a next-door neighbor for a while, you would learn to love her again."

The man groaned, "Sir, you don't understand what I'm saying. It's not that a romantic fire has gone out and I need a little space to get it ignited again. The fact is I can't stand the woman. I can't even bear the thought of even living in the same neighborhood with her."

"Ah," sighed the minister, "Now I understand. What you're saying is that your estrangement is so deep you are feeling hostile with her."

The man responded, "Bingo! Reverend, now you're catching on!"

The minister remained undaunted as he pursued his original course. "May I interpret your remarks to mean that you feel a deep-rooted enmity towards your wife?" The man allowed the inference. "Then," said the minister, "let me remind you that God commands us to love our enemies!"

Exasperated, the man walked away sorrowfully, shaking his head. How can one argue with a minister like that?[21]

GOD'S VIEW OF LOVE

God's view of love is very different from that of the world's. God gives us His definition of love in 1 Corinthians 13:4–8:

> Love is patient, love is kind. It does not envy, it does not boast, it is not proud. It is not rude, it is not self-seeking, it is not easily angered, it keeps no record of wrongs. Love does not delight in evil but rejoices with the truth. It always protects, always trusts, always hopes, always perseveres. Love never fails.

That description is what love is. You will not see or find a single mention of some "ishy-squishy" feelings that are here today, gone tomorrow. Actually, we could read it by inserting our names into it: "Henry is kind, Henry is patient..." and that would give us a better idea just what God sees as love.

Instead of seeing love as a feeling, we should see it as an action. Years ago, I came across an excellent definition of love: "Love is a commitment to have an attitude and do actions that are the best for someone else." We see this by the various Greek words that are used for "love." First, there is the Greek word "eros" which refers to sexual love. It is the root for the word "erotic." It is not used in the New Testament. Second, there is "stergos" which we could translate as "family love": the love a father has for his children and children for their parents. Third is "philein" which is the love we can have for a friend. The name "Philadelphia" comes from this and literally means "love for a brother."

The final Greek word is "agape" and it refers to a deep, sacrificial love. It is the word that John 3:16 uses: "For God so loved (agape) the world that He gave His only Son…" When you think of Jesus' sacrificial love for us, think of this: did He *feel* like going to the cross?

It is with this understanding of the meaning of love that Romans 13:8–10 instructs us:

> Let no debt remain outstanding, except the continuing debt to love one another, for he who loves his fellowman has fulfilled the law. The commandments, "Do not commit adultery," "Do not murder," "Do not steal," "Do not covet," and whatever other commandment there may be, are summed up in this one rule: "Love your neighbor as yourself." Love does no harm to its neighbor. Therefore love is the fulfillment of the law.

Love is an action, not a feeling.

LOVE IS A DECISION

Therefore, love in marriage simply means making a decision to start loving the other person by doing loving things for him/her. I once read about an African who was asked how arranged marriages in his country worked. He responded by saying, "You North Americans love a girl and then marry her; we Africans marry a girl and then love her."[22]

I recall a visit from a fellow who was unhappy in his marriage and he confessed to me about his wife: "I just don't love her!" Based on my understanding of love, I simply responded, "Then start!" As someone has so aptly stated, "Love is a daily decision."

You see, since love is commanded, then it can never be a feeling, for how can you control your feelings? Jesus said, "If you love me, keep my commandments!" (John 14:15). What are God's commandments? One of them is in Ephesians 5:25: "Husbands, love your wives." Another one is in Titus 2:4: "Older women (are) to teach the younger women to love their husbands." If there is anything that Jesus commands me to do, I can do it. He will never ask me to do what I cannot! So, if He commands me to love my husband, to love my wife, I *can* do it!

J. Allen Petersen writes how the newspaper columnist and minister, Dr. Crane, tells of a wife who came to see him, full of hatred towards her husband.

"I don't only want to get rid of him, I want to get even. Before I divorce him, I want to hurt him as much as he has me."

Dr. Crane came up with an ingenious plan. He instructed her, "Go home and act as if you really loved him. Tell him how much he means to you. Praise him for every decent trait. Go out of your way to be as kind, considerate, and generous as possible. Spare no efforts to please him, to enjoy him. Make him believe you love him. After you've convinced him of your undying love and that you cannot live without him, then drop the bomb. Tell him that you are getting a divorce. *That* will really hurt him."

With revenge in her eyes, she smiled and exclaimed, "Beautiful. Beautiful. Will he ever be surprised!"

And she did it with enthusiasm. Acting "as if" she loved him, for two months she showed him love, kindness, listening, giving, reinforcing, and sharing.

When after two months she didn't return, Dr. Crane called her. "Are you ready now to go through with the divorce?"

"Divorce?" she exclaimed. "Never! I discovered that I really do love him."

Her actions had changed her feelings. Motion had resulted in emotion.[23]

IT TAKES WORK

This approach to love, I must warn you however, is hard work. It's not easy. And not everyone is willing to work at it in that manner. Sometimes, people would rather not do what it takes to truly love their spouse.

A woman accompanied her husband to the family doctor for his yearly check up. After the examination, while the husband was getting dressed, the doctor called the wife aside for a consultation. He informed her that her husband was severely depressed, had lost his will to live and would surely die unless she followed his instructions to the letter. He then wrote out the following on a prescription pad and gave it to the wife:

1. Each morning, arise from bed before your husband and be sure to serve him a hearty breakfast. Let him read the morning paper without interruption and send him off to work in a good mood.

2. At lunchtime, make him a warm, nutritious meal. Do not bother him with household problems and put him in a good frame of mind before he returns to work.

3. For dinner, prepare especially nice meals with a gourmet touch, selecting his favorite foods. Do not nag him while he is watching sports on TV during the evening hours. Make sure the remote is handy at all times for him. Massage his back as he watches.

4. Make love to him several times each week and satisfy his every sexual whim and fantasy.

The wife read the list, put it in her purse and thanked the doctor for his advice. On the way home, the husband asked, "What did the doctor say to you during his consultation?" She replied, "He said you're gonna die!" While this story exaggerates my point, it does illustrate that, unfortunately, not everybody is willing to work at it.

Feelings of romance in a marriage do follow acts of love. Gerald Dahl writes, "When we begin to do the right, loving thing toward those we are commanded to love, whether we feel like it or not, God compensates by giving the feelings."

Love is not what someone else does to us. I once

had a fellow say to me of his girlfriend, "I really love her. She makes me tingle." My response to him was, "I don't think you do love her. I think rather that you love yourself. You love her because of what she does to you. So, your focus is on yourself and how she makes you feel, not on her." He looked at me, uncertain as to what to make of it.

Since love is an action, in the next chapter we will look at how to communicate love to your spouse, in one of five different ways.

LOVE IS OUR HOME

It has been over 35 years, since I looked across that room at Millar, and I can honestly say that I love my wife, Linda, more today than ever. I thought I loved her then, but today, I know I truly do love her. Because, in the words of the song by Sandi Patty, "Love is our home."[24]

> If home is really where the heart is,/ Then home must be a place that we all share./ For even with our differences our hearts are much the same,/ And where love is we come together there.
>
> Wherever there is laughter ringing,/ Someone smiling, someone dreaming,/ We can live together there, love will be our home./ Where there are children singing, where a tender heart is beating,/ We can live together there, love will be our home.
>
> With love our hearts can be a family,/ And hope can

bring this family face to face./ And though we may be far apart our hearts can be as one,/ When love brings us together in one place.

Wherever there is laughter ringing, someone smiling, someone dreaming./ We can live together there, love will be our home./ Where there are words of kindness spoken, where a vow is never broken./ We can live together there, love will be our home.

QUESTIONS FOR SMALL GROUP DISCUSSION

1. If you have children, share any stories you may have about their understanding of love, or use some stories you may have from your own childhood.

2. Most people would acknowledge that the world's essential view of love is that it is a feeling. What is the difference between infatuation and true love?

3. Were you surprised to learn that "romantic feelings of love last a little more than a year"? Or had you already discovered that in your own experience? How would that knowledge affect people's decisions in an affair?

4. Discuss God's view of love as an action. Is it really a decision we get to make? Can a person begin to love simply by a decision to do so? Does motion result in emotion?

5. Do you agree with Gerald Dahl's statement that "when we begin to do the right, loving thing towards those we are commanded to love, whether we feel it or not, God compensates by giving the feelings?" Have you had that experience in your own life?

6. It was stated, "This approach to love is hard work. It's not easy." Do you agree? But is it worth it? Why or why not?

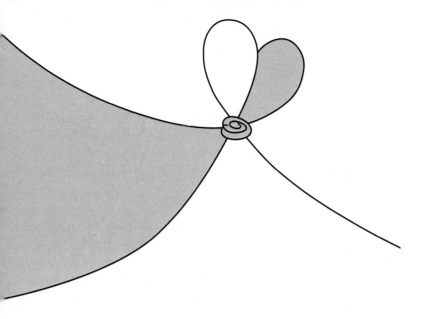

THIS, MY DEAR IS HOW I LOVE YOU!

We have all been created with the need to be loved and to have that love shown to us. One very unhappy wife dragged her husband to a marriage counselor to see if he could save their flagging marriage. The counselor listened to the wife as she went on and on about her husband's failure to love her. Finally, he had heard enough. He asked the husband, "Are you willing to do whatever it takes to save your marriage?" The husband sighed, "Yes, I am."

With that, the counselor stood to his feet, went to the woman and pulled her up from the chair she was sitting in. He put his arms around her and gave her a long, lingering kiss. The husband stared in amazement, and the wife was astounded. The counselor finished the kiss, turned to the husband and said, "If you want to save your marriage, your wife needs that at least twice a week!" "W-w-w-well," stammered the husband, "I guess I can bring her in on Tuesdays and Thursdays!"

Some years ago, I read about the research a king in medieval Europe did. He wanted to find out what language children would speak if they were never spoken to. He recognized that children brought up in homes where English was spoken would learn to speak English; those in French homes would speak French and so on. But he wanted to know if there was some universal language children would learn if there was no input from others.

So, he went to an orphanage and selected a number of children that he brought to his palace. He then instructed the nurses who took care of these children to feed and clothe them but to never speak to them or communicate with them. The king never did end up finding out what language children would innately learn. That's because all of the children in the experiment died! We need to have love communicated to us, if we are going to survive.

A pastor friend shared with me how for a period of time, while going to Bible College, he worked as an ambulance attendant. One day, they arrived at the scene of a suicide attempt of a young man. As they were transporting him to the hospital, my friend asked the young fellow why he had attempted to kill himself. His answer: "Because nobody loves me."

In marriages all across this land, you will find men and women frustrated, unhappy, and feeling very unloved. And not infrequently, you will also find a very perplexed spouse. Like the fellow who said to his pastor, "I can't figure my wife out! Why is she still so unhappy? I've worked so hard to provide for her everything she needs: nice house, nice furniture, money for clothes and so on. Yet she says that she doesn't feel loved!"

We have all heard that line, haven't we? Why is that? It is because we all communicate and receive love in very different ways. In his excellent book entitled *The Five Love Languages*,[25] Gary Chapman talks about the different "languages" people speak in love to each other. This chapter will build on that concept with some further applications from the experience I have had in this area. I have asked my wife, Linda, to help me explain some of the ways of communicating love which we all can use. The first one she will look at is acts of service.

ACTS OF SERVICE

In a very informal survey of a few women, I discovered that the most common answer to the question of what love language they wanted most was acts of service. A simple definition of acts of service would be: seeking to please one's spouse by serving him and expressing your love to her, by doing things for him. For husbands, actions such as cleaning up after a meal, vacuuming, wiping the sink clean after you shave, taking out the garbage, changing the baby's diaper, cleaning out her car, changing the cat's litter box, picking up the papers, and making the bed are all ways you can show your love.

You are probably saying to yourself—no problem, just let me know when you want me to do those things, and I'll do them. But the secret to real loving acts of service is not having to be told to do them. When wives need to ask for acts of service, then they are no longer acts of love, but simply response to requests or demands. When a spouse observes a need and responds on his own to meet that need, it is truly an act of love.

These actions require thought, planning, time, effort, and energy, and when a spouse does these things without being told, it communicates to his mate that he was thinking of how he could please her. He has studied her needs; he has understood her mental, emotional, physical state and realized that she needs a break. He has become a student of his wife's needs, and he understands what will best minister to her. As Peter writes, "You husbands in the same way, live with your wives in an understanding way, as with someone weaker, since she is a woman; and show her honor as a fellow heir of the grace of life, so that your prayers will not be hindered" (1 Peter 3:7, NASB-U). In doing so he communicates that he loves her.

Jesus gave a simple but profound illustration of expressing love in the last chapter of John when the disciples had been fishing all night and caught nothing. Jesus then told them to throw the nets out the other side of the boat. They did and caught many fish. When they reached land, it says that Jesus had a fire burning and breakfast was ready. This is a perfect example of an act of service: Jesus had prepared a meal for His hungry disciples.

Here's a little assignment: choose a simple but humble task that you may not especially like but know your spouse would be pleased to see completed. Surprise your spouse by doing it without being asked.

Now, Henry will look at physical touch.

PHYSICAL TOUCH

The second way we can communicate love is through physical touch. The need to be touched is innate in all warm blooded animals; it causes them to feel more comfortable and peaceful. When a person is touched, the amount of hemoglobin in the blood increases significantly. Hemoglobin is the part of our blood that carries vital supplies of oxygen to all organs of our body, including the heart and the brain. An increase of hemoglobin helps prevent disease and speeds recovery from illness. Researchers have documented the ability of touch to slow heart rate, lower blood pressure, and increase levels of serotonin, the brain chemical that's linked to well-being. It also decreases levels of the stress hormone, cortisol, and thus boosts immunity.[26]

When we are touched by someone, it communicates love. In Song of Solomon 8:3, the beloved says of her lover, "His left arm is under my head and his right arm embraces me." A free lance reporter from the *New York Times* was interviewing Marilyn Monroe years ago. She was aware of Marilyn's past and the fact that during her early years, Marilyn had been shuffled from one foster home to another. The reporter asked Marilyn, "Did you ever feel loved by any of the foster families with whom you lived?" "Once," Marilyn replied, "when I was about seven or eight. The woman I was living with was putting on makeup, and I was watching her. She was in a happy mood, so she reached over and patted my cheeks with her rouge puff...For that moment, I felt loved by her." When Marilyn said that, she had tears in her eyes. Why? The touch had lasted only a few moments but it made a lasting impression on her.

Communicating love through physical touch includes things like holding hands. For years, I watched as Albert and Irene, a couple in our church, would walk into the church from the parking lot, holding hands. I remember thinking, "How nice!" You communicate love by doing something as simple as holding your beloved's hand.

It is also communicated through hugging. Maybe you heard of the fellow who wanted to learn about hugging; so, he went to the library and got a book entitled *How to Hug*. When he came home, he found out it was book 12 in the Encyclopedia Britannica.

A third way is through casual touching. Small things like holding hands while waiting in line, giving an unrequested back rub, gently stroking the hair, and hugging tenderly all communicate love in a very real way to others.

Every husband should know that research has shown women need eight to ten meaningful touches each day to maintain a physical and emotional healthy state. Virginia Satir, family therapist says, "We need 4 hugs a day for survival. We need 8 hugs a day for maintenance. We need 12 hugs a day for growth."[27] I need to point out, however, that 80% of those touches must be non-sexual in nature. [28] One wife complained to me that the only time her husband touched her was when he wanted sex from her. She shared how, one Sunday morning in church, however, her usually untouching husband reached out and put his arm around the back of her chair. She went on a high that lasted several days, she told me.

Cathy McBride writes, "I remember one morning when I came face-to-face with the power of touch. That Sabbath we had a visiting speaker in our church and my husband, LeBron, sat next to me in the pew. A hectic week had left me physically and emotionally exhausted, and I felt about as significant as a discarded cigarette butt. Though I had blinked hard and tried to concentrate on the speaker, tears of discouragement burned my nostrils and threatened to overflow. Then, out of the blue, LeBron reached across the back of the pew, placed his arm around my shoulder and squeezed me to him. His touch transformed my attitude. Instead of feeling like a discarded cigarette butt, I felt more like a 20 carat diamond."[29]

Linda will share about another way of showing love and that is by spending quality time together.

TIME TOGETHER

Quality time happens to be my personal love language. This has changed somewhat from when the children were small and I was at home and later, when I was working outside the home. Then, I would have to say that my love language was acts of service. But now that my schedule has slowed down and there are only two of us at home, I no longer feel the need for as much help around the house. What I long for most now is meaningful conversation. This is an aspect of quality time. When we talk about quality time, we mean time spent focusing on each other. It's not when you sit together on the couch and watch TV–or worse yet, the hockey game! (Ouch! That hurt!–Henry).

It means giving undivided attention, looking at each other, talking, and listening to each other. For many people it's easy to talk, but when your talk time is over, the quality time is up. For true expression of quality time, listening is just as important as talking. It means listening with your mind and your body. That means you don't read the paper, fix the loose table leg, play with a pencil, or whatever. It means you look at the other person in the eyes and truly listen.

It means that you carve out time in the week to do something together. It may take the form of a walk together or something as elaborate as a weekend get away. The activity is incidental; the important thing is that emotionally we are focusing on each other. The activity is the vehicle that creates the sense of togetherness.

It means quality conversation—sympathetic dialogue where two individuals are sharing their experiences, thoughts, feelings, and desires in a friendly, uninterrupted context. You have probably heard others say or perhaps said yourself, "my spouse never talks to me." That doesn't mean they don't open their mouths and speak, it means that they seldom take part in sympathetic and meaningful dialogue.

Quality conversation is quite different from what Henry will write about next, "words of encouragement." That focuses on what we are saying, while quality conversation focuses on what we are hearing. It means that we will draw out our spouse through conversation. It means I will listen sympathetically to what you say. I will ask questions, not in a badgering manner but with a genuine desire to understand your thoughts, feelings, and desires. It means that you are free to say what you need to say, and I will not negate your feelings or challenge your statements.

If you are frustrated because you feel your spouse doesn't really understand you, listen to you, validate your feelings and thoughts, if you long for more time just simply being together, then perhaps your love language is "Quality Time."

Henry shares about the next way we communicate love—through words of encouragement.

WORDS OF ENCOURAGEMENT

Proverbs 18:21 says, "The tongue has the power of

life and death." Proverbs 12:25 says, "An anxious heart weighs a man down, but a kind word cheers him up."

A young mother, who had her five-year-old son with her, met a friend at the mall. As they visited, the little boy asked for some money for the drink machine. Before she gave him the money, she asked, "What do you say?" The little boy replied, "You're thin and you're pretty." He immediately got his money!

Another way of communicating love is by the words we say to each other, using words that build up your spouse. Mark Twain once said, "I can live for two months on a good compliment." Unfortunately, many spouses don't realize how important a word of love is. A wife complained to her husband, "You never tell me you love me!" "Listen!" he replied, "I told you I loved you 28 years ago at the altar and if anything changes, you'll be the first to hear!"

The language of love happens when we express appreciation: telling our spouse (and our children) that we appreciate them. Proverbs 31 tells about the "virtuous woman" (KJV) or the "excellent wife", as the NASB puts it. It says of her, "Her children praise her, and with great pride her husband says, 'There are many good women, but you are the best!'" (Proverbs 31:28–29, CEV). No wonder she was the amazing woman she was: she was receiving such powerful affirmations!

I like the story of the little boy who loved his mother and who loved to sit on her lap. One day, as he was sitting on her lap, she was reading a book to him. After she finished the book, he cuddled up close to her and said,

"I love you, Mommy!" His mother was grateful for his love but asked, "How can you love a mother who is fat and ugly?" The boy quickly responded, "Oh, Mommy, you are not! You're fat and pretty!" We communicate love when we encourage others with our words, though those words do need to be carefully chosen, for sure.

Finally, it happens through kind words: "A gentle answer turns away wrath, but a harsh word stirs up anger" (Proverbs 15:1). The tone we use is also so important. A loud, harsh word is not an expression of love but of judgment and condemnation. Years ago, at a pastor's seminar, we were being taught how to visit in people's homes. The speaker encouraged us to smile when we spoke to people. He said that if you smile while saying to another person, "I hate your guts!" that person would smile too and think to themselves, "He didn't say that!"

Another way to communicate love is through giving gifts. Linda will share about this:

RECEIVING GIFTS

If your spouse's primary love language is receiving gifts, you have it made. In fact, it is one of the easiest love languages to learn. Gifts can be purchased, found, or made. The husband that stops along the road side to pick a wild flower for his wife has just communicated to her that he was thinking of her: "Because you are special, I took the time to stop and pick this."

Gifts are visual symbols of love and they are very

important to the people who speak that language of love. For example, to some the wedding band is so crucial—it is the ultimate gift of love. As result, they will never remove the ring from their finger.

For those of you who do not speak this language, you may think that buying a flower that will die in a few days, or a card that will be read and then either put away or thrown out is simply a waste of money. Not so! Gary Chapman, who wrote the book *The Five Love Languages,* studied anthropology. He visited six different cultural groups on three continents and discovered without exception that an attitude of love always accompanied the giving of gifts. In particular, gift giving was a part of the love-marriage process.[30]

A gift is something you can hold in your hand and say "Look! She was thinking of me" or "He remembered me." It was not only just the thought, but the thought that spurred them to action. The best gift I ever received from Henry was a gold chain with a gold cross on it. He gave it to me when I began working as Director of Women's Ministries. He said that each time I traveled, he wanted me to wear it as a reminder that he was thinking of me and praying for me. Not only was that a delightful gift in and of itself, but all the thought that went into it and the meaning behind it makes it a cherished gift.

CONCLUSION

We think the exercise of determining your love language

is valuable within the marriage context. It is one more way to strengthen the marriage bond, to get outside of ourselves and the way we think, and to selflessly think of our mate. We encourage you to get together with your spouse and begin sharing with each other what you feel your love language is.

In attempting to discover your spouse's love language, it's important that you understand what your partner desires most. For example, you may have heard or perhaps even said yourself, "Well, I do things for my wife! Like yesterday, I cut wood for our fireplace. Isn't that an act of service? Why doesn't she get all excited about that?" We're sure she does appreciate it, but is that something that she herself would normally be required to do? Or is it something that you yourself usually do?

We suggest that you listen carefully to her conversations. Does she say things like, "I just don't have time to get to the vacuuming..." or "If someone would just make a meal for me sometimes...?" Those are clues as to what she really wants and needs.

Listen to your spouse's comments (and criticisms) about your behavior. That will provide you with the clearest clue as to her primary love language. People tend to criticize their spouse most loudly in the area where they themselves have the deepest emotional need. If we understand that, it may help us process their criticism in a more productive manner.

Now, the tendency that sometimes happens is to focus on giving love with the language we speak. So if, for me, love is expressed by physical touch, then I tend to express my love to my spouse with that language. And that's okay if touch happens to be her language, but if it's not, then I need to discover what her language is and use it for her, even if it feels unnatural to me.

That is what the case was with the fellow we began this chapter with, who said to his pastor, "I can't figure my wife out! Why is she still so unhappy? I've worked so hard to provide for her everything she needs: a nice house, nice furniture, money for clothes, and yet she says that she doesn't feel loved!" His love language may have been giving gifts and he was perplexed that his wife didn't think he loved her. But her love language may have been quality time. We saw that significantly illustrated in one couple we worked with. His language was acts of service (he cleaned up after meals, tidied up the house and so on in ways that made Linda drool.) But his wife was desperate for physical touch. They ended up, tragically, getting divorced because of this misunderstanding of each other's love language.

Let us emphasize this: it is a very unselfish act to love the other person with their love language not your own! But there is a big red flag we want to wave for you: do not focus on your own love language; focus rather on your mate's. In other words, don't develop this attitude: "You know what I want and need so do it!" Do something very selfless: focus on your mate's needs. We are human and very self-focused and our human nature will demand that our spouse meet our needs in *our* love language. But we would encourage you to do what God has instructed us to do in His word in Romans 12:10

where we are taught, "in honor preferring one another" (KJV).

We challenge you to show love to your spouse in *their* love language.

QUESTIONS FOR SMALL GROUP DISCUSSION

1. Tell a story of one time when you thought you were communicating love but the other person didn't see it that way at all.

2. Discuss each of the five ways of communicating love (acts of service, physical touch, time together, words of encouragement and receiving gifts). Give your own examples of times when you have given or received love in any of those ways.

3. Analyze yourself and decide what your love language is. Then study your spouse and determine what his or her love language is.

4. Discuss the statement: "We tend to focus on giving love with the language we speak." Have you experienced this? Is it true?

5. Discuss this statement: "It is a very unselfish act to love the other person with their love language, not your own." How difficult is it for you?

6. Answer this question, just to yourself: "Am I willing to show love to my spouse in his/her language, no matter how difficult it is for me?"

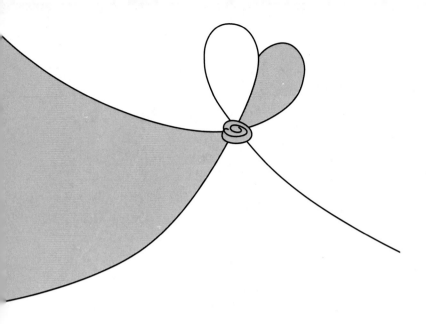

MORE JOY IN YOUR MARRIAGE

In some marriages, there isn't very much joy. One man became quite convicted about the fact that his marriage was not very good and that he had not been showing his wife the love she needed. He realized he had been neglecting her. So he left his office, went to the florist shop, and bought a dozen red roses. Then he went to the drugstore and picked up a bottle of cologne, as well as a box of chocolates. He had the chocolates wrapped, and he sprayed himself liberally with the cologne.

Then he drove home, stood at the front door, and rang the doorbell. His wife answered the door and taking one look, burst into tears. She sobbed and sobbed until her now distraught husband was finally able to calm her down.

"What's wrong, honey?" he asked. "Why are you crying?"

"Oh," she said, "You won't believe the day I've had! First, Billy sprained his ankle at school, and I had to take him to the hospital. Then the dog dug up all the flowers I had just planted in the flower bed. Then the washing machine broke down, and I had to take the clothes to the Laundromat. Then your mother phoned and said she was coming to stay with us for two weeks, and she talked and talked and talked until I burned the supper.

"Now," she wailed, "you come home drunk!"

The Bible gives us much teaching on marriage and how it can and should be a joyful experience. Our master teacher is Jesus, and His views are positively enlightening on the subject of how to have more joy in your marriage.

MORE JOY THROUGH BEING "ONE FLESH"

One day, Jesus was approached by the Pharisees and asked about His position on divorce. They asked, "Is it lawful for a man to divorce his wife for any and every reason?" (Matthew 19:3). But before He gave His teaching on divorce, Jesus gave His teaching on marriage. In the creation, He said, God "made them male and female" (Verse 4). This shows us that God's original intention for marriage was not be a "same sex" affair:

God "made them male and female" indicates His intention for marriage to be heterosexual in nature. As someone has stated, "It was to be Adam and Eve, not Adam and Steve."

Then He went on to say that marriage is leaving: "For this reason a man will leave his father and mother" (Verse 5a). We are to cut both the apron strings and the purse strings from mom and dad. I have often said that each premarital counseling class should have both sets of in-laws there to clarify this new role, both for the sake of the young couple and their parents. More on this in the chapter on in-laws, later.

Third, marriage is cleaving: "and be united to his wife" (Verse 5b). In marriage, a new, higher relationship is established and it is that of husband and wife.

Finally, marriage is becoming one flesh: "and the two will become one flesh. So they are no longer two, but one. Therefore what God has joined together, let man not separate" (Verse 6).

What does it mean to become "one flesh?" Part of that is obviously referring to sex and I will address that topic later. Another aspect of that is that it is to be monogamous. Now, polygamy is found in the Old Testament, but, like divorce, it was allowed but not approved.

But there is more to the idea of becoming "one flesh" and this chapter will explore it in greater detail.

ONE FLESH MEANS COMPLEMENTING

When the Bible says married people become "one flesh", it means the marriage is to be complementary, not competitive. When God created Eve and brought her to Adam, He called her a "helper suitable" for him. The word translated in English as "helper" is, in Hebrew, "ezer." This means that Eve was one who provided for what was lacking in Adam. She did for him that which he could not do alone. This does not suggest that, as one guy put it, "Before marriage, a man is half a man; after marriage, he is finished."

Eve was to help Adam by being there, talking things over with him, giving love and care, sharing joys and perplexities, ideas, fears, sorrows and disappointments. Eve was designed to complement, to add that feminine dimension to Adam and make him into a well-rounded person. Indeed, every wife does that to her husband. You can so easily see the difference between married men and bachelors in this regard.

OPPOSITES ATTRACT

Second, the word "suitable" suggests one who corresponds to, one who complements us. This is the reason why we tend to marry opposites. We have all heard the cliché that opposites attract. It's true: God wired you in such a way that there is an inborn instinct in you that causes you to naturally gravitate toward people who complement you, who are not exactly like you. It is natural that very structured people tend to be fascinated and drawn toward people who are unstructured and spontaneous. And people who tend to be shy and quiet are fascinated and drawn toward people who are outgoing and boisterous.

OPPOSITES ATTACK

While it's true that opposites attract, it is also true that after you are married, opposites attack. What used to be fascinating is now frustrating. Tim Lahaye writes of a woman who after 13 years of marriage asked him, "What makes people like us marry in the first place? We have a hopeless personality conflict! Both of us can be relaxed and gracious when around others but when together, we bring out the worst in each other."[31]

Because of this "opposite" aspect, too many marriages take on the mindset of a world heavyweight boxing match. It is him against her: they tend to think in terms of "winning," of beating the other person. But if you think in your marriage in terms of "I won" or "she or he won," then you have already lost. A marriage based on competition will have continual conflict. "If a house is divided against itself, that house cannot stand" (Mark 3:25).

On the other hand, I really believe God loves to put opposites together. Rick Warren says, "I think it is His sense of humor. For instance, are you an early riser? You probably married somebody who's a night owl who stays up late and doesn't believe in God before 11:00 a.m.! Perhaps you are daring and impulsive. You most likely married someone who is cautious and reserved.

One of you loves to talk. The other is a bump on a log. Those who love to spend money married tightwads. It happens inevitably. Those who love to cuddle married a porcupine. I believe it is through those challenging contrasts that we grow and become the stronger people He wants us to become."[32]

COMPLEMENTARY MARRIAGE

God's plan is for marriage to be complementary, not competitive. He desires that they have emotional oneness; that they see themselves as one flesh. It is not: "mine" and "his" or "mine" and "hers;" it is: "ours." In a complementary marriage, there are goals they have both agreed upon in prayer for their marriage and they work together for the achievement of those goals. Years ago, I met Audrey and Pete. What was interesting was that Audrey would refer to the various items they owned as "my car" or "his fridge" and so on. I remember thinking that was not a good basis on which to build a strong marriage.

In a complementary marriage, each thinks in terms of what is good for the marriage, not what is good for themselves. A Biblical example of complementariness is Aquila and Priscilla. Of them, the Apostle Paul writes, "Greet Priscilla and Aquila, my fellow workers in Christ Jesus. They risked their lives for me. Not only I but all the churches of the Gentiles are grateful to them. Greet also the church that meets at their house" (Romans 16:3–5). This couple became a powerful force for good as they worked together, complementing each other, in their service for God.

Now, becoming one flesh may mean making lots of adjustments. Too many couples enter marriage in a sort of hazy romantic bliss with their eyes blinded by love. Benjamin Franklin said, "Keep your eyes wide open when you get married and half shut afterwards." Marriage is taking two, often very different, individuals with contrasting personalities, abilities, tastes, and dreams and bringing them together. Unfortunately, that can then be like the irresistible force meeting the immovable object. To fuse them together into a working unit may, in many cases, require a lot of (sometimes) painful adjustments. Like the guy who said, "I thought I was marrying Raquel but I got Rosanne!" Another woman said, "I thought I was marrying Mr. Right, but I didn't know his first name was Always!"

Becoming one flesh means recognizing this and conscientiously working at making those necessary adjustments. And that is often with a lot of give and take—mostly give! "Be devoted to one another in brotherly love. Honor one another above yourselves" (Romans 12:10).

Much of that adjustment happens in the first year of marriage. It can be as simple as learning to live with someone who squeezes the toothpaste tube in the center, instead of rolling it up, as it should be! (Actually, the way to resolve that is to have two toothpaste tubes...)

I think back to our first few years of marriage. Take the matter of eating out in restaurants. The way I saw it, the only time you ate at a restaurant was when you were away and couldn't make it back home. Even then, you would not necessarily go to a restaurant. That is what my parents did. Coming from a Ukrainian background, you always went to a "Ukrainian McDonald's." A "Ukrainian McDonald's" was where you went to the grocery store, bought a ring of garlic sausage, a loaf of bread and something to drink! Then you went to the car and ate it there. Besides, it was a lot cheaper that way, too. Then I met Linda. She's sophisticated. She likes the finer things of life including fancy restaurants (and, I realize, they are expensive!) So initially, we never went out. But then I gradually began to see what it meant to Linda and so I tried it once. I enjoyed it. Now I thoroughly enjoy it! By the way, if you are looking for somebody to take out, we're available.

ONE FLESH MEANS COMMUNICATING

A golden anniversary party was thrown for an elderly couple. The husband was moved by the occasion and wanted to tell his wife just how he felt about her. She was very hard of hearing, however, and often misunderstood what he had to say. With many family members and friends gathered around, he toasted her: "My dear wife, after 50 years, I've found you tried and true!" Everyone smiled in approval but his wife said, "Eh?" He repeated louder: "*After 50 years I've found you tried and true!*" His wife harrumphed and shot back, "Well, let me tell you something: after 50 years, I'm tired of you too!"

A good marriage is one where there is good communication. It is where a lot of talking takes place. Indeed, good communication is one of the major keys to a happy marriage. Communication creates a sense of belonging and acceptance: if I open up to you and share with you my innermost thoughts, it shows that I consider you to be a valuable part of my life. This was the complaint that Delilah had against Samson: "How can you say, 'I love you,' when you won't confide in me?" (Judges 16:15).

Good communication takes time, effort and practice: it usually doesn't just happen. I personally make it a part of my schedule to spend several hours each week just talking to Linda: on my days off, at lunch, when I'm home in the evenings. Our signal is the word "coffee?" which one of us will ask the other. Both of us will then stop what we are doing, get a cup of coffee, and talk together. For myself, throughout the day I try to remember things to share with her. If I see or hear something interesting, I think, *I'll have to tell Linda!* It is a priority in my life to communicate because I know how important it is to our marriage.

As a Christian husband, I try to follow the mandate of 1 Peter 3:7 to live with my wife in an understanding way. That means, through communication, I get to know her needs, deep fears, cares, disappointments, expectations, secrets, dreams and such. A good husband asks his wife questions, probes, discovers her deepest self. I once heard someone use the analogy of a potter who runs her fingers around the rim of the pot she has just made, feeling for cracks in the new pot. In the same way, a careful husband will run his fingers around the rim of his wife's soul and will seek to discover what cracks need to be found and covered up. Someone has said, "Rare is the husband who spends time and thought coming to an understanding of his wife's needs."

It is true that some men struggle with communication in their marriage. One husband said to me: "I'm naturally non-communicative!" There are many reasons men have communication problems. Some men are too wrapped up in themselves, too pre-occupied with their own issues. For others, it is the fact that communication techniques are not always automatic, and need to be learned. For still others, there is the tendency to take one's wife for granted and they put little effort into pursuing the meeting of her needs. They are simply unwilling to make a commitment or the effort to work at it.

MARRIAGE COSTS

The truth is it costs to have a great marriage. It costs a lot in time, effort, and energy. But it costs even more to divorce. There are financial costs, emotional costs, relational costs, physical costs, memory costs, etcetera. You leave a part of yourself with that person when you divorce. You may divorce but you will never be totally free because you gave them your life. If you have kids, you are never going to be totally free from that person.

Yes, it costs. But it is far more worth the cost to save the marriage and let God make it a miracle marriage than it is to just chuck it!

Rick Warren asks, "What do you do when you do not feel like working on your marriage? You pray and obey. You pray, 'God, give me the feelings again.' And obey. You decide, 'I am going to do the right thing whether I feel like it or not.' That is a mark of maturity. Immature people go around saying, 'I don't do what I don't feel like doing.' That is immaturity. Be a person of character. Do the right thing whether you feel like it or not. Most of what gets done in the world is done by people who don't feel like doing what they are doing but still do it anyway! Show some courage. Have some class. Build some character. Do the right thing whether you feel like it or not. And God will bless it."[33]

Dr. James Dobson recently included a letter he received from a listener to his radio program, "Focus on the Family," in his monthly newsletter. In it, a young woman, Jacquie, tells her experience: "I was married to a non-believer for 14 years in what proved to be a living hell on earth. There's no way I can describe how terribly Brent treated me during that time. I considered running away or anything that might help me cope. It seemed that my prayers and my church work were useless in bringing me peace of mind. Gradually, I gave in to the advances of another church member. He was also unhappily unmarried and inevitably, we became deeply involved in an affair."

"This man's wife then died of heart disease, and I

intended to divorce my husband to marry him. But when Brent saw he was losing me with no hope of reconciliation, he quietly gave up all the terrible treatment of me and became kind, almost overnight. He even changed occupations to give him more time at home."

"That put me in a very difficult situation. I loved the other man and felt I couldn't live without him and yet, I knew it was wrong to divorce my husband. By an act of sheer faith, I broke off the relationship with the other man and did what I believed to be right in the eyes of God. For three years, I did not feel anything for my husband. I claimed the scriptures and believed that if I would do what they said, the Lord would give me what I never had. I admit that I went through a terrible struggle with my emotions at this time."

"During the last two years, however, God has poured out a blessing on us that you can't believe! I am so committed to my husband that I find myself loving the man that I hated for 14 years. God has given me this intense affection for him. Now, something else has happened. Our children have grown so close to us and love each other as never before. We love to look in the scriptures for things to obey and then we make a commitment to do what we've read. First, it included a daily study of the Word and now it involves church work—together. We are a witness to all those who see this incredible change in our family."

"I said all that to say this: it is worth everything to follow God's will, even when it contradicts our desires. Oh, there's always the temptation to chuck it all, from time to time. But I'd rather spend five minutes in real fellowship with the Lord than a lifetime in fun and games. I can truly say it works!"[34]

ONE FLESH MEANS VALUING

Being one flesh means that we place the highest priority on each other, as husband and wife. That means the husband does not take his wife for granted, and she does not take him for granted either. I once wrote in my weekly column in our local paper, "We should love people and use things. Too often, unfortunately, we love things and use people." As result, I had a fellow who made a special appointment to come in and see me because he was so touched by it. "People, not things!" he kept saying, over and over.

A mother watched as her little boy smashed a toy he was playing with into her dining room table, making a mark in it. The father was incensed and was about to tear into the child for his childish act, but she intervened. "No way!" she said, "I'm not going to let you ruin my $3 million dollar child for a $300.00 table!" People are more important than things.

When we place that high priority and value on our spouse, then we will make a special effort in several areas. First, we will attempt, on a regular basis, to connect with each other. We live such busy lives, too busy, that relationships suffer. But when we value our spouse, we will spend quality time with them so they can feel they are loved. I like the Old Testament command to newly married husbands: "If a man has recently married, he must not be sent to war or have any other duty laid on him. For one year he is to be free to stay at home and bring happiness to the wife he has married" (Deuteronomy 24:5). How neat is that? Can you imagine the positive impact that would have on marriages if we followed it today?

I find it interesting to note that numerous studies have found that the most important issue to people facing death is their relationships with those they love. Rarely do the dying express regret over money, business opportunities, personal appearance, or public achievements. Again and again, the dying person is desperately concerned with his/her relationships: "Have I said what needed to be said? Does she know I loved her? Is he still angry with me?"

Make sure that when it comes to dying, you won't have any of those regrets because you made sure you put all the effort you could into bringing more joy into your marriage.

QUESTIONS FOR SMALL GROUP DISCUSSION

1. Share with your group about one of the happiest days in your marriage so far. What was it that made it so happy for you? Could that be repeated?

2. Discuss the concept of becoming "one flesh" in marriage. How does that relate physically, emotionally and spiritually?

3. Have you observed the reality of the statement that, in marriage, opposites attract? Do you know some couples where this is evidently the case? Is it true in your case?

4. What about the statement that "opposites *attack*." Have you seen cases where this is also true? Why does that which used to be fascinating become frustrating?

5. How important is communication to a marriage? If it is important, what practical things can every couple do to see that it actually happens? What kinds of things block good communication?

6. Do you agree with the statement "it costs to have a great marriage?" What are some of the costs you have noted?

7. How can we value our spouse? What are some practical ways to do so?

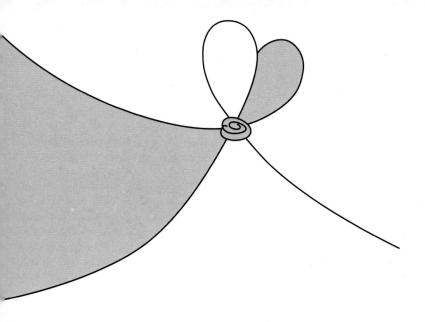

SEX AND THE CHRISTIAN COUPLE

A manufacturing company received a form from the government asking for a statistical analysis of its work force. The president asked his secretary to fill it in for him. When she returned the finished survey back to him, he noted one of the questions was: "How many employees do you have, broken down by sex?" She had written as her response: "We don't know. Most of the problems here are alcohol related."

We live in a sex saturated society. Kids today, at age 10, know more about sex than did couples on their wedding night four decades ago. We do not need more information on the mechanics of sexuality. We have more than enough explicit information available. What is lacking today is an accurate understanding of God's purposes in sex and also a willingness to obey those, thereby finding the greatest possible satisfaction that God intended from it.

In this chapter, I want to provide you with that understanding: an attempt to correct some of that misinformation you may have received along the way.

WRONG BELIEF #1 ABOUT SEX: "SEX IS SINFUL."

Some people have been taught that sex is a necessary evil. It is necessary for the procreation of the human race but otherwise, it is sinful. Even the great church theologian, Augustine (354–430 AD), complained about God's creation of sex. He didn't like it, he said, because it had "animal like movements." He wrote, "Marital intercourse for the sake of procreation has no fault attached to it, but for the satisfying of lust, even with one's husband or wife, for the faith of the bed, is venially sinful; but adultery or fornication is mortally sinful. Moreover, continence from all intercourse is even better than marital intercourse itself, even if it takes place for the sake of procreation."[35]

I heard of one pastor who announced in church that he and his wife were adopting a child. Someone from the congregation was heard to respond, "That's how *all* pastors should have children!" To that person, there was just something inherently *wrong* with a pastor having sex with his wife.

To people who think like this, sex came as a curse on the world, the result of sin. The cult leader, William Branham, who is still followed by many today, said that sex was the cause of the fall into sin in Genesis 3. Sex was the forbidden fruit Satan used to tempt Eve with. He said that she had sex with the serpent and subsequently, she tempted her husband and he similarly fell into sin.[36]

THE VICTORIANS AND THE PURITANS

Rick Warren suggests that much of this comes from our legacy of the Victorians. Now, unfortunately, many people confuse the Puritans with the Victorians. The Puritans were the people who settled America and from whom we get the idea of Thanksgiving in autumn. But the Victorians were the uptight people who lived in England during the reign of Queen Victoria (1837–1901). It was the Victorians who, for example, covered piano legs for the sake of modesty. But the Puritans, on the other hand, were not uptight about sex. The godlier they were, the more sensual they were. He says, "I read where a woman once came to a Puritan pastor and then to the church to complain that her husband was not making love to her and the church voted to excommunicate him out of the church." He goes on to say, "I wonder what would happen to the churches in America if we did that today."[37]

SEX GLORIFIES GOD

But sex is not only not sinful, but rather, when a husband and wife engage in it, it glorifies God. A mother was explaining the facts of life to her little daughter. She listened attentively for a while and then asked, "Does God know about this?" He certainly does, and He entirely approves of it. Indeed, one entire book in the Bible, the Song of Solomon, is all about marriage and sex. As you read it, you realize that sex is something that God has created. He planned it for our enjoyment as husbands and wives. He smiles in approval when He sees us doing what He has created us to do.

1 Timothy 4:4 says, "For everything God created is good, and nothing is to be rejected if it is received with thanksgiving." Note the word, "everything." The Bible says that everything God created is good. Does that include sex? Yes, it includes your sexuality. Sex is part of what God made you to be.

So, sex is not sinful. It is not even a necessary evil. It is the perversion, the misuse, the abuse of sex that is wrong. But sex, in its rightful place between a husband and a wife, is exactly what God created. We should accept it without guilt and without shame. It's not dirty, not bad; it's actually a sacred activity. "Honor marriage, and guard the sacredness of sexual intimacy between wife and husband. God draws a firm line against casual and illicit sex" (Hebrews 13:4, Msg).

Sex has profound spiritual implications. That is why you are to reserve it for marriage only. "May your fountain be blessed, and may you rejoice in the wife of your youth. A loving doe, a graceful deer—may her breasts satisfy you always, may you ever be captivated by her love" (Proverbs 5:18–19).

Note the word "captivated." That word is one of the strongest verbs in the entire Hebrew language. It can be translated, "be intoxicated," and even "let your mind be blown away..." One translation says, "Let her steal away your senses." That's the Bible talking about sex. God's ideal for sex in marriage is that it is fun and fantastic. That is very different from the way most people think the Bible teaches about sex.

In 1 Corinthians 6:20, we read, "Use every part of your body to glorify God" (TLB). It says "every part." God didn't make some parts of your body good and some parts evil. Rather, every part of our body is good. We were created to have sex.[38]

GOD CAN HEAL SEXUAL HURTS

I also recognize that few areas can create more hurt, disappointment, frustration, and bitterness than the area of sexual relations. It creates a lot of conflict. There is a lot of hurt and confusion about sex because people have misused, abused, perverted, and exploited it. I am sure there is a lot of hurt even among those reading this book.

But God is the great healer even in this area of our lives. I recently prayed with someone who was sexually abused as a child, and the healing God brought was amazing. If that is your case, come to God in prayer and let His love heal you in this very important part of your life. Psalm 145:3 says, "He heals the brokenhearted and binds up their wounds." You may even need good Christian counseling. Be sure this gift God has given you is one you can truly enjoy.

WRONG BELIEF #2 ABOUT SEX: "SEX WITH ANYONE IS OKAY."

There are other people who believe that sex is just another appetite, like hunger, that should be satisfied. This is probably the dominant view in our society today. The basic assumption of many sex education advocates today is that kids *must* satisfy their drives, and that abstinence will produce neurotic frustration. But let me suggest that this idea is actually an insult to young people. When they are being told, "You can't control your urges," they are actually being told, "You are no more than a dog!" From my kitchen window, I recently watched our neighbor's dogs, doing what God created dogs to do. Now, I am not surprised that they were; it is their nature. They *can't* control it. But a human being, created in the image of God, has the power and ability to control his or her urges. Galatians 5:22–23 says, "But the fruit of the Spirit is...self-control." Young people are not like dogs.

Sex, according to the Bible, is reserved for marriage only.

> Is it a good thing to have sexual relations? Certainly—but only within a certain context. It's good for a man to have a wife and for a woman to have a husband. Sexual drives are strong, but marriage is strong enough to contain them and provide for a balanced and fulfilling sex life in a world of sexual disorder.
>
> 1 Corinthians 7:1–2, Msg

Though some people see this as a negative (they think it as repressive), in reality it is a positive. A while back, *Redbook* magazine took a survey of women all across America and they discovered that the greater the intensity of a woman's spiritual convictions, the more likely she is to be highly satisfied with the sexual pleasures of her marriage. "In other words, sexuality and spirituality go together...The most sexually fulfilled women were the most spiritual women..." is the study's conclusion. [39]

CHURCH LADIES ENJOY SEX MORE

Some time ago, I wrote in my weekly column in our local paper about a study done by researchers at the University of Chicago. I entitled it, "Church Ladies Enjoy Sex More" and quoted William R. Mattox Jr. as saying this was the most "comprehensive and methodologically sound" sex survey ever conducted. He said that the results showed that "religious women experience significantly higher levels of sexual satisfaction than do non-religious women."

"First," he writes, "church ladies appear to benefit from their lack of sexual experience before marriage."

That is because most Christians promote saving sex for marriage. This pays considerable dividends according to David Larson of the National Institute for Healthcare Research. He says, "Couples not involved before marriage and faithful during marriage appear to be more satisfied with their current sex life than those who were involved sexually before marriage."[40]

Secondly, Mattox writes that "churchgoers appear to benefit from a commitment to marital fidelity and marital permanence." This is because, according to sex therapist Mary Ann Mayo, "Mutual commitment to lifelong marriage...makes it easier for women to 'let themselves go' sexually...their sexual responsiveness is greatly affected by the relational context in which love making takes place."[41]

A third reason is because, according to a 1982 UCLA study, sexual satisfaction is positively affected by the "absence of sexual promiscuity, of the fear of AIDS and other sexually transmitted diseases and of the fear of getting caught or the fear of rejection. They are also free of guilt because they are not violating their own sexual standards."[42]

Sexual activity is always best in the context of a permanent, long term relationship—where it is not ridden with guilt, fear of discovery, of unwanted pregnancy, STD's etc. As the Song of Solomon puts it in 2:16: "My lover is mine and I am his…"

WRONG BELIEF #3 ABOUT SEX: "IT'S ALL ABOUT ME AND MY NEEDS."

Some people see sex from a very selfish perspective. The classic Biblical illustration is that of Amnon who used Tamar for his own indulgent purposes in 2 Samuel 13:6–14. But the same can happen in marriage too. It is for this reason the Bible describes sex in marriage as being dictated by the needs of the other, not oneself. When you married, you gave your partner the right to your body. If you did not want to do that, you should not have gotten married. That is part of what marriage is about. "Two will become one" (Matthew 19:5) is the way the Bible phrases that.

As a husband or a wife, you are to use your body to meet the sexual needs of your mate.

> The marriage bed must be a place of mutuality—the husband seeking to satisfy his wife, the wife seeking to satisfy her husband. Marriage is not a place to 'stand up for your rights.' Marriage is a decision to serve the other, whether in bed or out."
>
> 1 Corinthians 7:3–5, Msg

This is the exact opposite of what the world teaches: "How much can I get and how soon can I get it?" It is all selfish. A couple was getting ready for bed and the husband brought his wife a glass of water and an aspirin. "What's that for?" she asked. "I don't have a headache." The husband pointed at her and said, "Aha! Gotcha!"

The Bible says we are to understand our spouse and what his/her needs are. For example, a husband needs to learn what makes his wife "tick." 1 Peter 3:7 says, "You husbands, likewise, live with your wives in an understanding way" (NASB). He needs to understand her, including things like moods, headaches, and hormones.

WHAT WOMEN WANT?

Unfortunately, some men are very "clued out" about their wives and their needs. Like the fellow who went to a marriage seminar with his wife. The instructor addressed the men about their need to understand their wives. "Men," he asked, "Can you describe your wife's favorite flower?" The husband leaned over, touched his wife's arm gently, and whispered, "It's 'Pillsbury All-Purpose' isn't it?"

At the same time, men tend to find that women are quite complex. Sigmund Freud himself confessed, "The great question that has never been answered, and which I have not yet been able to answer, despite my thirty years of research into the feminine soul, is 'What does a woman want?'" [43]

Recently, I came across a story that illustrates the struggle men have in understanding women. According to this story, King Arthur was ambushed and imprisoned by the monarch of a neighboring kingdom. The monarch could have killed him but was moved by Arthur's youth and ideals. So, the monarch offered him his freedom, as long as he could answer a very difficult question. Arthur would have a year to figure out the answer and, if after a year, he still had no answer, he would be put to death.

The question? "What do women really want?" Such a question would perplex even the most knowledgeable man, and to young Arthur, it seemed an impossible query. But, since it was better than death, he accepted the monarch's proposition to have an answer by year's end.

He returned to his kingdom and began to poll everyone: the princess, the priests, the wise men and even the court jester. He spoke with everyone, but no one could give him a satisfactory answer. Many people advised him to consult the old witch, for only she would have the answer. But the price would be high, as the witch was famous throughout the kingdom.

The last day of the year arrived and Arthur had no choice but to talk to the witch. She agreed to answer the question, but he would have to agree to her price first. The old witch wanted to marry Sir Lancelot, the most noble of the Knights of the Round Table and Arthur's closest friend! Young Arthur was horrified. She was hunchbacked and hideous, had only one tooth, smelled like sewage and made obscene noises. He had never encountered such a repugnant creature in all his life.

He refused to force his friend to marry her and endure such a terrible burden. But Lancelot, learning of the proposal, spoke with Arthur. He said nothing was too big of a sacrifice compared to Arthur's life and the preservation of the Round Table. Hence, a wedding was proclaimed and the witch answered Arthur's question thus: "What a woman really wants," she answered, "is to be in charge of her own life." Everyone in the kingdom instantly knew that the witch had uttered the truth and that Arthur's life would be spared. And so it was. The neighboring monarch granted Arthur his freedom and Lancelot and the witch had a wonderful wedding.

The honeymoon hour approached and Lancelot, steeling himself for a horrific experience, entered the bedroom. But, what a sight awaited him. The most beautiful woman he had ever seen lay before him on the bed. The astounded Lancelot asked what had happened. The beauty replied that, since he had been so kind to her when she appeared as a witch, she would henceforth be her horribly deformed self only half the time and the beautiful maiden the other half.

Which would he prefer? Beautiful during the day or during the night? Lancelot pondered the predicament. During the day, he could have a beautiful woman to show off to his friends, but at night, in the privacy of his castle, would he be satisfied with an old witch? Or, would he prefer having a hideous witch during the day, but by night, a beautiful woman for him to enjoy wondrous intimate moments?

A question for the guys: What would *you* do? What Lancelot chose is below. But make your choice before you keep reading.

Noble Lancelot said that he would allow her to

make the choice herself. (He was a good listener!) Upon hearing this, she announced that she would be beautiful all the time because he had respected her enough to let her be in charge of her own life.

Now, what is the moral to this story? The moral is: If you don't let a woman have her own way...things are going to get ugly!

SEX BEGINS IN THE MORNING

Doug Fields tells how he went to premarital counseling with his fiancé before he got married. He says, "I don't remember very much. But I do remember a couple of things. One, the counselor said, 'Sex starts in the morning,' I'm thinking, *'All right!'* But," Fields goes on to say, "what he meant was, it starts in the morning with how you wake up and begin to treat one another. It took me about three years to figure that out."[44]

Sex happens all day. It is the kind words, the little notes, the call on the phone, the flowers, the caress and loving look, the affirming word. In the atmosphere of affection, there is a set up for the sexual relationship.

One of the common complaints I have heard from women about their husbands and sex: they often feel "used." "After being ignored all day by my husband, then I am expected to jump into bed at night and be all excited to have sex?" complains one wife. "I just can't do it!" One of the causes of so much "frigidity," of wives being unresponsive to their husbands sexually, is the simple fact of the husbands not understanding their wife's need for love and attention all day long.

If men gave women the affection they craved, they likely would get more of the sex they desire.

WHAT MEN NEED

A good wife will also learn what makes her husband "tick." The fact of the matter is that most men are turned on by sight. Indeed, there is a chemical reaction that happens in every man's body when he sees an attractive woman. In 2 Samuel 11:2–3, we read: "One evening David got up from his bed and walked around on the roof of the palace. From the roof he saw a woman bathing. The woman was very beautiful, and David sent someone to find out about her." All it took for David to get turned on was Bathsheba's naked body. Someone has said, "Men are kind of like light switches. You can turn them on pretty quick. You just flip the switch and the light turns on. Sometimes the light is on but nobody's home. But the light is still on. Women on the other hand, are more like irons. They warm up slowly. They do get hot, but it takes a while." Another analogy I've heard is that men are like microwaves and women are like crock pots. Men are always ready for sex, women warm up more slowly. It takes *t-i-m-e*.

Realizing that is the way men are, means, as a guy, you have to discipline your eyes not to lust (that is difficult in today's environment but not impossible.) Martin Luther wrote about this male temptation and suggested that while "you can't stop the birds from flying over your head, you can stop them from building a nest in your hair." As a young man, I remember asking an older, godly Christian man how he dealt with this in his life. He said to me, "Henry, whenever I see a pretty girl, instead of fantasizing about her, I pray for her." I remember thinking, *"That man is giving me, as a red blooded male, good advice!"*

WITHHOLDING SEX

Never manipulate by withholding sex from each other. The Bible is very clear that when you withhold a sexual relationship from your wife or your husband because you are angry at them or because you are too busy or simply because you are not interested, that that is sin.

> Do not cheat each other of normal sexual relations, unless you both decide to abstain temporarily to make special time for prayer. But afterwards, you should resume relations as before, or you will expose yourselves to the obvious temptations of Satan.
>
> 1 Corinthians 7:5, Ph

Sex is never to be used as a weapon or reward. Perhaps, some of you are thinking, *I just don't ever feel like it.* Rick Warren says, "As a pastor, I would say to you, 'Find out why.' Find out why you don't feel like it. There may be a hundred legitimate reasons for that. It could be biological or hormonal. It could be as simple as you are too tired because your schedule is too heavy. It could be unresolved conflict, childhood sexual abuse, or any number of a hundred legitimate reasons. But every one of them can be solved. Do not let your marriage die because of that. When you ignore your mate's sexual needs, you are setting yourself and also setting them up for sexual temptation. That is very dangerous thing to do. Let me use an analogy: when you go on a diet, how often do you find yourself thinking about food? If you are like me, it is probably a lot more than when you are not on a diet. It is like that is all you can think about. This also happens when you deprive your mate of a normal sexual relationship. That is especially true for a man because of the way he is wired up biologically. When a man or a woman is satisfied at home, most of the time they will not go looking elsewhere."[45]

CONCLUSION

The goal is to create a magnet in your home. "Enjoy the wife you married as a young man. Lovely as an angel, beautiful as a rose—don't ever quit taking delight in her body. Never take her love for granted!" (Proverbs 5:18–19, Ph). Martin Luther put it this way: "Let the wife make her husband glad to come home and let the husband make her sorry to see him leave."

Make the decision: "If my husband/wife is going to have a great lover, it's going to have to be me!" If you do not, I guarantee you Satan will gladly create a magnet in the world for your mate.

Begin to work on it today. I challenge you to commit yourself to working on this, praying about it, getting whatever help you need to the point that your husband/wife would say "I would be a fool to give this up." Make your marital grass so green, everyone else's looks brown. As one man put it, "Why would I ever be interested in a used clunker on the street when I've got a Mercedes at home in the garage? Why eat hamburger out when I've got steak at home?"

May that be true for you.

QUESTIONS FOR SMALL GROUP DISCUSSION

1. Respond to St. Augustine's complaint that sex was not good because it contained "animal-like movements." Do you think God was wrong in choosing to create sexual activity in the way He did? Why or why not?

2. Discuss the statement, "sex glorifies God." Why do we often think we need to separate the idea of sex and God?

3. Obviously, some people abuse sexuality and so it becomes the source of much pain in some people's lives. How can God heal sexual hurts?

4. People often use the analogy that you would not buy a car without trying it out first, so why try marriage without having sex first? Is restricting sexual activity to just married people a good thing to do? Or is it "repressive," as some people claim? Why is sexual activity best experienced within the bounds of the marriage relationship?

5. Analyze the study by researchers at the University of Chicago which said that "religious women experience higher levels of sexual satisfaction than do non-religious women." Discuss the various reasons why they state that this is so.

6. Can husbands and wives both react selfishly towards sex in their marriage? How?

7. Doug Fields' counselor made the statement, "Sex begins in the morning." Why is this important to the wife? Why should it be important to the husband?

8. What is one way that men can discipline their eyes to not lust?

9. Just by yourself, think on this: "If my husband/wife is going to have a great lover, it is going to have to be me." Make the decision that that is what you will do.

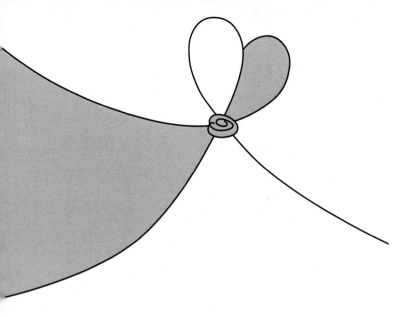

IN-LAWS AND OTHER OUTLAWS

A Bible study group was asked what they would do if they had just four weeks left to live. One man said he would go and try to lead as many people to Christ as possible in his town. Another said she would dedicate her life to serving her family, church, and fellowman. A third said he would take his family, along with his mother-in-law, and travel all over the county in a Ford Escort and stay in a Motel 6 every night. "Why in the world would you do that?" he was asked. "Because that would be the longest four weeks of my life!"

Many people have a negative attitude towards their in-laws. Perhaps you heard of the fellow who brought his dog to the vet and asked him to cut off its tail.

"Why?" asked the vet. "Because my mother-in-law is coming this weekend," the man replied, "and I don't want her to think she's welcome!"

Even someone as full of integrity as Abraham Lincoln had in-law problems. Of them, he said, "The Todd's are very important people. They require two d's at the end of their name. The Almighty is content with one."

Someone once asked me, "What is the difference between in-laws and outlaws?" After I responded that I didn't know, they replied, "Outlaws are wanted." Roger Slick puts it, "If marriages were outlawed, only outlaws would have in-laws."

There are few relationships that get as much negative press as in-law relationships. On most evenings, my wife and I try to relax at the end of a busy day by watching some comedy on TV. For a while, we enjoyed the humor of *Everybody Loves Raymond* and particularly the bizarre antics of Frank and Marie, the parents of Raymond and in-laws of Debra. They, particularly Marie, are constantly interfering in Raymond and Debra's matters, driving Debra to distraction. Watching some of her antics reminded me of the comment someone made that if you rearrange the letters in "mother-in-law", it actually spells "woman Hitler." A while ago, I was listening to the "oldies" radio station and the song by Huey Lewis and the News called, "Mother-in-law" came on:

Mother-in-law, mother-in-law, the worst person I

know,/ Mother-in-law, mother-in-law. She worries me so./ Mother-in-law, mother-in-law, If she leaves us alone, we could have a happy home./ Sent from down below, mother-in-law, mother-in-law./ Satan should be her name, Mother-in-law, mother-in-law./ To me they're about the same. Mother-in-law, mother-in-law.[46]

When it finished, a female D.J. made a personal comment. She said she felt the song was simply "perpetuating the stereotype." But, in-law relationships have been the cause of many a family fight and even divorces.

What does the Bible say about the matter of in-laws? You might find it interesting to note that of the 12 disciples, the only one that has his mother-in-law mentioned in the Bible is Peter, whom some have suggested was the first Pope (Mark 1:29–31). And then there was Solomon. Some have envied Solomon because he had 300 wives and 700 concubines. However, they have found their enthusiasm to follow in his footsteps tempered when they realized he also had 1000 mothers-in-law! Comedian Robert G. Lee says, "If you think you've got problems, just remember Solomon had over one thousand wives and concubines. Do you have any idea how many birthdays and anniversaries he had to keep straight?"

In this chapter, we want to look at this crucial relationship and what the Bible has to say about it.

THE PRINCIPLE OF LEAVING

The Bible teaches that when a man marries a woman, he is to leave his father and mother. "For this reason a man will leave his father and mother and be united to his wife, and they will become one flesh" (Genesis 2:24). In the Biblical context, the woman automatically left her father's house to come to her husband's. We see this in the case of Rebekah in Genesis 24:57–61. When the servant of Abraham came to find a wife for his master's son, Isaac, it was Rebekah who left her father, Bethuel's, home in Aram Naharaim to go and live with her new husband in Canaan. It was always the man who brought his wife to his home.

This is the imagery that Jesus uses for His bride, the church, to whom He promises, "In my Father's house are many rooms; if it were not so, I would have told you. I am going there to prepare a place for you. And if I go and prepare a place for you, I will come back and take you to be with me that you also may be where I am" (John 14:2–3).

But the husband who still physically lived with his parents was to "leave" them in the sense that he now had a new, higher relationship and commitment: his new wife. Marriage is therefore leaving. It means cutting the father's purse strings. A man seeks to become independent economically. The story is told of a young woman who brought her fiancé home to meet her parents. After dinner, the father invited the young man into his study for a talk. "So what are your plans?" the father asked the young man. "I am a Biblical scholar," he replied. "A Biblical scholar, hmmm..." said the father. "Admirable, but what will you do to provide a nice house for my daughter to live in?" "I will study," the young man replied, "and God will provide for us."

"And how will you buy her a beautiful engagement ring, such as she deserves?" "I will concentrate on my studies," the young man replied. "God will provide for us." "And children?" the father asked. "How will you support children?" "Don't worry sir, God will provide," replied the fiancé. The conversation proceeded like this and each time the father questioned, the young idealist insisted God would provide. Later, the mother asked her husband how it went. The father answered, "He has no job and no plans and he thinks I'm God."

Besides cutting the father's purse strings, it also means cutting the mother's apron strings, that is, becoming independent emotionally. Too many marriages have been destroyed because these strings were still attached. More than once, I have had wives coming to me absolutely grief stricken over the husband's relationship with his parents. In two cases I am thinking of, the young couple lived on the same yard on the farm, as did the parents. In both cases, my counsel to them was, "Move!"

Sometimes, the "leaving" is a command the wife needs to obey. One lady told me she had a fight with her new husband shortly after she was married and she called her Mom and Dad and told them, "I'm coming home!" "Oh no, you're not!" her mother had said to her. "It was the best thing she could have done," she later reported to me. A marriage where one or the other is overly dependent on one's parents is an unhealthy marriage.

THE PRINCIPLE OF CLEAVING

In the King James Version, Genesis 2:24 is translated, "Therefore shall a man leave his father and his mother, and shall cleave unto his wife: and they shall be one flesh." The word "cleave" there suggests the fact that the new couple form an entirely new entity. They are to become "one flesh."

That means the couple are united in several different ways. First, they are united emotionally. From this point on, they see themselves, not as "I" but as "we." Second, they are united physically. As result, they live together in the same house. Third, they are united sexually. One flesh pictures the act of sexual intercourse. In 1 Corinthians 6:16–17, Paul writes, "Do you not know that he who unites himself with a prostitute is one with her in body? For it is said, 'The two will become one flesh.' But he who unites himself with the Lord is one with him in spirit." And, finally, it means they are united spiritually. In God's sight, He looks at the new couple and sees them as one.

That means the marriage relationship now transcends the parent-child relationship. This was the case for Rebekah and Isaac in Genesis 24:67: "Isaac brought her into the tent of his mother Sarah, and he married

Rebekah. So she became his wife, and he loved her; and Isaac was comforted after his mother's death."

THE PRINCIPLE OF LETTING GO

While the principle for couples marrying is leaving, the principle for parents is letting go. In my experience, many marriage problems have been caused by parents who refused to let their children go. In fact, I would say more marriage problems are caused by parents who refuse to let go than by children who refuse to leave. The problem is parents who hang on.

Howard Hendricks gives wise counsel to parents to let go. I heard him say, as a seminary professor, "We often have fellows coming to the seminary holding their umbilical cord, looking for a place to plug it in!" He went on to say, "Parents! Let go! And when they leave, sing the 'Hallelujah Chorus!'"

In our church, before we will perform a marriage ceremony, we require premarital counseling, with at least a three month's lead-time before the actual wedding itself. Otherwise, there will be no marrying. We see that as very important. But I have often said that one session should be with both sets of parents to set a few ground rules, with the principle of letting go being the primary focus.

Parents need to follow the advice given by Paul in 1 Thessalonians 4:11, to "make it your ambition to lead a quiet life, to mind your own business." Parents need to learn how to keep out of their married children's business.

GOOD IN-LAW RELATIONSHIPS

The Bible gives us illustrations of both good and bad in-law relationships. A good in-law relationship is that of Naomi and Ruth in the book of Ruth. Naomi and her husband and their two sons moved to Moab to get away from a famine. There, Naomi's two sons married local girls by the names of Ruth and Orpah. (You may be interested to know that this was to have been the real name of the popular talk show host, Oprah. However, a spelling mistake occurred when her birth was being registered and it was changed it to Oprah.)[47]

Unfortunately for Naomi, both her husband and two sons died while in Moab. So, after the death of her sons, she sent both of her daughters in-law away, saying, essentially, don't feel obligated to me. Remarry and start all over again. While Orpah left, Ruth chose to stay and makes a statement of commitment, loyalty, and devotion to her desolate mother-in-law that has become a classic:

> Don't urge me to leave you or to turn back from you. Where you go I will go, and where you stay I will stay. Your people will be my people and your God my God. Where you die I will die, and there I will be buried. May the Lord deal with me, be it

ever so severely, if anything but death separates you and me.

Ruth 1:16–17

When Linda and I were married, this statement of Ruth's was part of Linda's wedding vows to me. It has always had an emotional impact on me whenever I read them. Ruth returned with Naomi to Israel where she met another man by the name of Boaz, married him, had a son who eventually became an ancestor of King David and ultimately, of Jesus Himself. This is an illustration of a good in-law relationship. But, unfortunately, there are also bad in-law relationships in the Bible.

BAD IN-LAW RELATIONSHIPS

A young fellow went to see his girlfriend's father for permission to marry his daughter. "I understand that you want to become my son-in-law," said the father to the young man. "No, sir, not really," the young man answered, "but if I want to marry your daughter, I don't see how it can be avoided."

One bad in-law relationship recorded in the Bible is that of Laban and Jacob, found in Genesis 29. It begins as an uncle-nephew relationship and, at first, a good one. Jacob had run away from his brother, Esau's, anger at him for stealing his birth right. Laban had hired him to work for him. Jacob had seen Laban's good-looking daughter, Rachel, and made a deal with him: seven years of work to marry her. In today's economy, that would be like paying $250,000–$300,000. That's fair coin, I think you would agree. I remember thinking initially that would be great for today. My son-in-law, Kevin, who is an American, would have had to pay me, a Canadian, that in U.S. dollars! But then I realized I have three sons, and they'd probably come to me for the money to help pay for their wives so I would be no further ahead, maybe behind.

But the father-in-law/son-in-law relationship soon degenerates. It begins with Laban's deceptions in his business dealings with Jacob and it continues with Jacob's success that prompts anger from Laban's sons. "Jacob heard that Laban's sons were saying, 'Jacob has taken everything our father owned and has gained all this wealth from what belonged to our father.' And Jacob noticed that Laban's attitude toward him was not what it had been" (Genesis 31:1–2). It climaxes with Jacob's decision to secretly leave, which he does. "Then Jacob put his children and his wives on camels, and he drove all his livestock ahead of him, along with all the goods he had accumulated in Paddan Aram, to go to his father Isaac in the land of Canaan" (Genesis 31:17–18).

Sometimes, the best thing for in-law relationships is being more than three hours away. I remember telling Linda that I was glad that, for the first few years of our married life, both sets of our parents were over three hours away from us.

CONCLUSION

We have the choice: our in-law relationships can be harmonious like Naomi and Ruth's was. Or they can be a constant struggle like Jacob and Laban's was. If we follow the basic principles of leaving and letting go, we will be well on our way to a good in-law relationship.

After that, it is simply following the Biblical command of how to get along in any relationship at all: "If it is possible, as far as it depends on you, live at peace with everyone" (Romans 12:18).

I first met my in-laws in the final year of my time at Millar, and I recall my first conversation with Roy, my father-in-law. He said to me, "Henry, when you take a girl on a date to a restaurant, say to her, 'You can have anything you want, fatso!'" I remember thinking, *Okay. Is this his way of telling me to leave his daughter alone?* I'm still not sure, and I don't intend to ask him.

But for the past 35 years that Linda and I have been married, I have had a wonderful relationship with her parents. I must honestly say that I have never had a day's conflict with them. They are wonderful, godly people. They have provided a rich heritage to me and to my children over the years, and I thank God for them.

One of the saddest days of my life was on May 7, 2006, when I sat in a hospital room in Dauphin, Manitoba, and watched as my mother-in-law's spirit left her body to go to be with Jesus. As I held my sobbing wife in my arms, I too wept as I thought of the wonderful mother she had been to Linda, the wonderful grandmother to my children, and the wonderful mother-in-law to me.

I only pray that, if you have had or will have in-laws, it will be as good for you as it has been for me.

QUESTIONS FOR SMALL GROUP DISCUSSION

1. What TV sitcoms, songs, or other media messages have you seen that reinforce the viewpoint (stereotype) that in-law relationships are always bad?

2. Discuss the statement from the Bible, "The two will become one flesh." Do you agree that it means they are united spiritually and in God's sight, that He looks at the new couple and sees them as one?

3. Why is the Biblical command to "leave father and mother" so important to the success of a marriage?

4. Why is the necessity of parents to "let go" also so important for the well-being of a marriage?

5. What was it about Ruth's attitude towards her mother-in-law Naomi that made it such a good relationship? What lessons can we learn from her and her mother-in-law?

6. What were the reasons that Jacob and Laban did not enjoy a good in-law relationship? What things did they do that caused such conflict and unhappiness? What lessons can we learn from them?

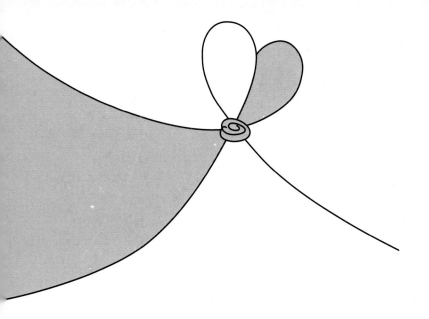

HOW COME THERE'S SO MUCH MONTH AT THE END OF THE MONEY?

Two guys were out golfing.

"Say, did I tell you my credit card got stolen three months ago?" asked the first one. "No," replied the other, "Did you report it?"

"No, I didn't," responded the first guy.

"Why not?" queried the second. "Because," he said, "right now, the thief is spending a lot less than my wife used to!"

According to a recent Gallup Poll, 64% of all couples argue over money. Finances are a major issue of concern in marriages. Some have gone as far as to say that it is the number one cause of divorce. Whether or not that is correct, financial disagreements still do create many problems in marriage.

The wisest man who ever lived was King Solomon. The scriptures say he "was greater in riches and wisdom than all the other kings of the earth. The whole world sought audience with Solomon to hear the wisdom God had put in his heart" (1 Kings 10:23–24). He wrote a book of wisdom called Proverbs, in which he gave a number of excellent principles for handling money. I am convinced that if these principles are followed, it will help overcome much marital conflict in this area.[48]

GOOD RECORDS – THE PRINCIPLE OF ACCOUNTING

Solomon wrote, "Be sure you know the condition of your flocks, give careful attention to your herds; for riches do not endure forever, and a crown is not secure for all generations" (Proverbs 27:23–24). In those days, Israel was an agricultural economy. Nearly everyone raised animals like sheep, goats, and cattle. Solomon's grandfather Jesse owned sheep and his father David was a shepherd boy. As result, he knew it was important to keep a close eye on one's cattle and sheep: things like disease or animals of prey could quickly ravage a flock.

In the same way, you can lose your money fast if you are not keeping close watch over it. We have all heard people saying, "I just don't know where all my money goes!" If you yourself have ever said that, it may be a warning light that you are in, or headed for, financial trouble. That may be because you are not keeping good records.

It has been said, "Money talks." I say it does not talk; it just sneaks away quietly. It does not tell you it is leaving. One fellow put it this way: "Riches may have wings but all I get to see are the tail feathers." Another guy said: "I have enough money to last me for the rest of my life; just as long as I die by the day after tomorrow..."

When it comes to keeping good records, you need to know at least two things. First, you need to know what you owe; that is your debt. And second, you need to know where it goes; that is, where you are spending it. Both husband and wife should know these important things. Many couples experience problems when one partner keeps the other partner in the dark about the finances. That is a recipe for financial disaster and for marital discord.

You may be saying you do not have the time to keep records. Let me ask you a question: Do you have time to worry? If you have time to worry about your finances, you have time to write it down. In fact, if you kept better records, you probably would have a lot less to worry about.

The Bible says riches disappear fast. Know the condition of your flocks. Know the state of your finances. This is the principle of accounting.

PLAN YOUR SPENDING – THE PRINCIPLE OF BUDGETING

Solomon also wrote: "The plans of the diligent lead to profit as surely as haste leads to poverty" (Proverbs 21:5). This is the principle of budgeting, of planning your spending.

Begin by setting godly financial goals and sticking with them. Too many people simply drift along, spending whatever they have but not according to any plan. Financial freedom is not based on how much you earn. It is based on how you spend it. If you were to make twice as much as what you make today, but if you were spending more than you are making, you would still be having financial problems.

Notice Solomon wrote, "Haste leads to poverty." One type of haste that leads to poverty is impulse buying. Impulse buying is essentially unplanned buying. It is based on emotions, on buying without thinking. There have been many times when I have gone into a store with no intention of buying anything. Then I saw something and bought it. Then I would go home and begin to think, *Now, why on earth did I buy this? Where am I going to get the money to pay for this?* I had bought it impulsively. I remember my dad buying something he really did not need, some "widget" he would likely never use. I asked him why he had bought it. "But, oh Henry, it was such a good deal! Actually," he proudly proclaimed, "I bought two!"

The Bible says, "Stupid people spend their money as

fast as they get it" (Proverbs 21:20, TEV). I once talked to a fellow who worked out on an oilfield where the guys worked hard all week and got paid on Friday night. This fellow said there were guys on his crew who had all their pay cheque spent by Sunday morning (and that wasn't by putting it into the offering plate at the local church).

If you are spending everything you have as fast as you get it, Proverbs 21:20 has a word for that: "stupid." We could also say, "dumb" and "not smart!" The New International Version translates that verse: "A foolish man devours all he has."

Spending can be just like any other addiction. Recently, a magazine article entitled, "Are you a shopaholic?" wrote, "Compulsive spending is a full fledged addiction just like gambling, alcoholism, and taking drugs." The Bible says this was part of the problem of the Prodigal Son: "The younger son packed his bags and left for a distant country. There, undisciplined and dissipated, he wasted everything he had..." (Luke 15:13, Msg).

Rick Warren says "It has become such a prevalent addiction in our society that there are organizations such as 'Debtor's Anonymous' and 'Shopper Stopper' set up to deal with it. These organizations come up with all sorts of creative ways to help people break the impulsive buying habit. They suggested to one lady that she keep her credit cards in a bowl of water in the freezer. Then, if she got the urge to spend, she would have to wait for them to thaw first. By then, they said, the urge would have passed and hopefully her sanity would have returned!" [49] Warren says he told this story to his congregation. Later, he received a letter from a fellow in his church. The letter said, "Pastor Rick, a certain husband in our church buried his wife's credit cards in the cement of the new room addition because ice cubes melt..."

How do you break the habit of impulsive buying and of spending more than you've got? You establish a budget. A budget is simply planned spending. A budget is telling your money where you want it to go, rather than wondering where it went. Everybody needs a budget. If you want to break this habit of spending more than you have, if you want to build resistance to sales and to impulsive buying, you need to set up a budget. Every Christian should follow a budget and use the spiritual fruit of self-control to stick with it: "The fruit of the Spirit is...self-control" (Galatians 5:22).

Shortly after Linda and I got married, we began to have financial struggles. We initially had this system: we would get our pay cheque, and then we would go shopping, usually spending most of our money in the first couple of days after getting our cheque. The result was that, frequently, we didn't have enough to last the month. I would be asking myself, "How come there's so much month at the end of the money?"

So one day we sat down and wrote down all our regular expenses: tithe, groceries, car expenses, hydro, telephone, golf green fees, water and sewer. We figured out how much we needed in all the areas of our family life for a whole year. Then we divided that by 26: the pay cheque that I received every second week. Then I got about two dozen envelopes and wrote the name of each on it: tithe, groceries, telephone, green fees for golf, hydro, etc. On each envelope, I also wrote how much I needed to put into it from each pay cheque so that in the course of the year, we could meet those expenses.

Linda got a plastic container and we put all the envelopes into it. Then we put it in the freezer part of our fridge. (I used to say, "We have *cool* cash!") Whenever we had to pay a bill, I would go to the fridge, get the appropriate envelope, and pay for it. Now, I realize the risk involved in having a bunch of cash in your fridge: it could be stolen. But I found it was a lot less risky having it there where thieves may possibly break in and steal than from my own impulsiveness.

That system helped me to discipline my impulsive nature: if there was no money in the envelope, I didn't spend it (in emergencies, I would borrow from another envelope but I always disciplined myself to pay the other envelope back). Sometimes we found we had to adjust the amount we were putting in a particular envelope to meet our current need (like upping our grocery envelope to feed three teenaged boys).

But it set us on the path to a financial stability that we never had before.

I recognize in this day and age where we are rapidly becoming a "cashless" society, with most of our expenditures done by credit cards, direct debit, pre-authorized cheque withdrawals, and such, that my system has become antiquated (though I still follow it to a lesser degree). But the principle of establishing a budget and following it still stands, no matter what system you use. I had one fellow say that I should still recommend to couples that, if this is what it takes to get your finances in control, then perhaps you *should* consider using the envelope system!

SAVE FOR THE FUTURE – THE PRINCIPLE OF SAVING

Solomon went on to write, "The wise man saves for the future..." (Proverbs 21:20, TLB). I read recently that the average Japanese family saves 25% of their income and the average European family saves 18% of their income. But the average American family saves only 5% of their income. Many people have absolutely no savings whatsoever, living from pay cheque to pay cheque. Why? It is because we are spending it all to keep up with the Jones'. And they've just refinanced but we are still trying to keep up with them. As a result we are not saving anything. But the Bible says, "The wise man saves for the future" (Proverbs 21:20, TLB).

The American Demographics magazine recently stated that most baby boomers are going to be flat broke in retirement. They are going to be in far worse condition in retirement than their parents are right now because they are not saving anything. "The reality of America's aging population, at this point, shocks no one. Still, as Baby Boomers near retirement age, one remaining 'gorilla-in-the-living-room' topic is the nation's capacity—or rather, incapacity—to deal with 75 million people, or 26 percent of the U.S. population, *avalanching into a 20- to 30-year life stage with prospects of low to zero income.*[emphasis added]"[50]

Why do we not save for the future? Why do we spend all that we get? I saw a billboard for a bank some time ago that said, "Jesus Saves. So should you!"

God intends for us to save money. "Lazy people should learn a lesson from the way ants live. They have no leader, chief, or ruler, but they store up their food during the summer, getting ready for winter" (Proverbs 6:6–8, TEV). It is the principle of setting a little aside so you are prepared for the financial storms that may come along. That is legitimate, intelligent financial planning. Save for the future.

At the same time, He does not want us to get involved in "get rich quick" schemes. "Wealth from get-rich-quick schemes quickly disappears; wealth from hard work grows" (Proverbs 13:11, NLT). Proverbs says over and over that money that comes easily disappears quickly. Instead, we are to faithfully work hard to earn it. "He who works his land will have abundant food, but the one who chases fantasies will have his fill of poverty" (Proverbs 28:19). "Committed and persistent work pays off; get-rich-quick schemes are rip-offs" (Proverbs 28:20, Msg).

In my opinion, that includes gambling. Many people are always waiting to win the lottery. There is a word for people who play the lottery: "Loser!" Each time we walk past the kiosks in the mall where lottery tickets are sold, I nearly have to restrain Linda. For the life of her, she simply cannot figure out how people can take their hard earned money and just throw it away. Frequently, you will see them standing by a trash can, ripping open their tickets and throwing the unlucky ones (almost always that means all of them) away. She said she feels like going up to them and asking, "Just give the money to me! I'll put it to good use!"

Rather, we are told to save it up. "He who gathers money little by little makes it grow" (Proverbs 13:11). This is talking about consistent, regular savings. "There is precious oil and treasure in the house of the wise. But a foolish man swallows it all up" (Proverbs 21:20, NASB).

I am not a perfect money manager but let me use another illustration from my life that you might find helpful. A number of years ago, I bought a small second car that I heard was very fuel efficient. It turned out to be a lemon; I had to make constant repairs on it and it became very expensive for me to own and run. My Dad later said to me, when I was complaining about this "economical" car, "Well, Henry, if you want economy, you have to pay for it!"

So, I sold it. When I got rid of it, we went back to just one car but I decided to keep on making the same payments I had been making, but now to a savings account. When it came time that I needed another car, I had enough saved up so I could pay for it in cash. Through the years, I have kept on doing that: making payments in advance. When I need to buy a car, I have the money saved up. During that time, I am also collecting interest, not paying it!

RETURN 10% TO GOD – THE PRINCIPLE OF TITHING

Solomon also wrote: "Honor the Lord with your wealth, with the firstfruits of all your crops; then your barns will be filled to overflowing, and your vats will brim over with new wine" (Proverbs 3:9–10). If there is one area that people struggle with in their finances, it is the idea of giving money to the church. Probably no area creates more negative attitudes than the idea that we should give away part of our hard earned money, especially to the church where corruption and scandal are rife (or so they claim...).

Yet, God Himself instituted the principle of tithing. It was His idea. He teaches that, as a part of good financial strategy for every couple, they should be tithing. There are three reasons for that:

A STATEMENT OF GRATITUDE

When I give away 10%, I am making a statement of gratitude about my past. Whenever I tithe, I am saying, "God, I realize that all I have comes from You in the first place, and if it wasn't for You, I wouldn't have anything!"

One woman shared with me that, after she became a Christian, she began the habit of praying before meals.

One day, her husband, who did not share her spiritual values, said to her, after she and her daughters had finished praying, "The only person around here who should be thanked is me!" She asked me what she should have said in response to him. I suggested that she ask him, "Who gave you the power and ability to earn the money in the first place? God did. If He wanted to, He could lay you low with one fell swoop. You would be flat on your back unable to walk or talk or earn even a penny!"

This is the attitude Moses warns about. "You may say to yourself, 'My power and the strength of my hands have produced this wealth for me.' But remember the Lord your God, for it is he who gives you the ability to produce wealth..." (Deuteronomy 8:17–18). So, in gratitude, realizing that even my very ability to work and earn money comes from God, I give to God 10%. When I give, I am saying, "I am not an ungrateful person. I am very grateful for what You have given me. Here is 10% in return." If I say I am grateful, but I do not tithe, then I am not grateful.

A STATEMENT OF PRIORITY

Secondly, whenever I give away 10%, I am making a statement about my present: a statement of priority. Whenever I tithe, I am saying, "God, I want You to be Number One in my life, so right from the top, the first part of my money goes back to You."

"Honor the Lord with your wealth, with the firstfruits of all your crops..." (Proverbs 3:9). Note the word "*first*fruits." That suggests that God is Number One. In Biblical times, before the farmer harvested the rest of crop, he made sure God got His portion. It was called "firstfruits." By doing so, he was making a statement of priority.

If before paying any other bills, I give to God first, I am saying that He is more important to me than anyone and anything else in my life. Someone once said to me, "We haven't tithed for a while. We decided God can wait so we paid the other bills first!" My response was to say that if I got some extra money and if the first thing I did with that money was to buy another golf club, what would that say be saying about my priorities? Notice that I did not say that I used it to buy a fishing rod or a rifle (or take my wife out for supper, or buy her a gift certificate for her favorite store, the Gap). What would I be saying? I would be saying that I am not into fishing or hunting or keeping my wife happy, either! I am into golf!

Somebody has said, "Show me your cheque book and your daytimer, and I'll tell you what's important in your life!" So, if I say that God is most important, but I am not tithing, then He is really not number one in my life. "The purpose of tithing is to teach you to always put God first in your lives" (Deuteronomy 14:23, TLB).

A STATEMENT OF FAITH

Whenever I give away 10%, I am also making a statement about my future: a statement of faith. We all have all sorts of bills and financial pressures, and we sure could use that money to take care of them. But, when I tithe, I am saying, "God, I am giving You this first tenth, believing that You will take care of me in the future." I am saying that I believe Philippians 4:18–19 when it says, "And my God will meet all your needs according to his glorious riches in Christ Jesus."

Normally, the Bible says, "Do not put God to the test!" For example, Deuteronomy 6:16 says, "Do not test the LORD your God as you did at Massah." But then we read God's promise in Malachi 3:10: "'Bring the whole tithe into the storehouse, that there may be food in my house. Test me in this,' says the Lord Almighty, 'and see if I will not throw open the floodgates of heaven and pour out so much blessing that you will not have room enough for it.'"

I call this the "Pepsi Challenge" of the Bible. God is saying, "Test Me, put Me to the test! See if I will not keep My promise to take care of you. Tithe." If you have not tithed, I urge you to begin now and say to Him, "Okay, God, I will give You 10% and see if You do keep Your promises." You might as well find out now if God is faithful or not. If He's not, you shouldn't waste the rest of your life following Him.

As we follow the instructions of 1 Corinthians 16:2, "On every Lord's Day you should put aside something from what you have earned during the week, and use it for this offering. The amount depends on how much the Lord has helped you earn", it becomes a weekly reminder to us: "God, You are first in my life!"

I should remind you, God does not need your money or mine. Why not? He does not need it because He owns it all already. But you and I need to give because of what it represents. As Jesus put it, "For where your treasure is, there your heart will be also" (Luke 12:34). God wants what it represents: our hearts. When we give Him our tithes, it shows Him He also has our heart.

Many couples having financial problems would find that those problems would largely disappear if they learned this principle and applied it.

ENJOY WHAT YOU HAVE— THE PRINCIPLE OF CONTENTMENT

The final piece of advice from Solomon is from Proverbs 19:23: "The fear of the LORD leads to life: Then one rests content, untouched by trouble." One of the greatest causes of financial mismanagement is the inability to be satisfied with what you have already. "It is better to be satisfied with what you have than to always want something else" (Ecclesiastes 6:9, GN).

Rick Warren says:

> There are four phases of discontentment. First, your yearnings exceed your earnings. So you go out and find a house (or car or boat or whatever) you really want. You can't afford it but you want it. Second, you overextend yourself financially because you're reaching for something a little too high. Third, as a result, you're overextended and you have to constantly hustle to make ends meet. Finally, after year

after year of hustling, family life begins to deteriorate. Everybody is exhausted. Everybody gets cranky. You don't have time for each other, much less time for the kids. We frequently rationalize our excessive, work driven lifestyle, by saying "It's a temporary condition. We're just doing this for a while. When we get caught up, then things will settle down." Unfortunately, this temporary condition quickly becomes a habitual lifestyle.[51]

The greatest challenge this presents is to the destructive effect it has on family relationships. Marriages deteriorate when we live at that breakneck pace. We need to learn to enjoy what we have and stop wanting more. "Be content with what you have" (Hebrews 13:5). Warren goes on to tell of a time when they had a family picture taken. "We were posing for it and the photographer said to one of my sons, 'Why don't you put your hand on your dad's shoulder? It'll look natural.' I said, 'If you want it to look natural, have him put his hand in my pocket.'" [52]

The Bible teaches we will never ultimately be satisfied by things. "Why spend money on what does not satisfy?" (Isaiah 55:2). The greatest things in life aren't things. Why do things not ultimately satisfy? Oh, they do for a while. You purchase a new item and you really like it. But six months later, it's not new anymore. The novelty has worn off: we've gotten bored with it. We want something new again.

But things do not satisfy. No *thing* is ever going to satisfy you ultimately. That is because, at the core of our beings, is a need that only God can satisfy—not money, not things. "If I have put my trust in money, if my happiness depends on wealth...it would mean that I denied the God of heaven" (Job 31:24, 28 TLB).

Blasé Pascal, 17th century scientist, who studied and identified barometric pressure wrote, "There is a 'God-shaped vacuum' in the heart of every man, and only God can fill it." He went on to say, "Man tries unsuccessfully to fill this void with everything that surrounds him, seeking in absent things the help he cannot find in those that are present, but all are incapable of it. This infinite abyss can be filled only with an infinite...object... God Himself."[53] Pascal here perfectly describes our secular culture in its futile search for fulfillment apart from God. Augustine, fourth century church father, wrote in his book, *Confessions,* of his search. He said, "My sin was this, that I looked for pleasure, beauty, and truth not in Him but in myself and His other creatures, and the search led me instead to pain, confusion, and error." Augustine's search eventually led to the discovery that God was the true object of his need: "Thou hast created us for Thyself, O God, and our hearts are restless until they rest in Thee."[54]

If you are feeling the pressure of finances in your life today, it may be a symptom of a deeper problem. If you are spending it all and saving nothing, and if you find yourself, as a couple, constantly arguing about this issue, that is a warning light of a deeper problem. It has been said, "Out of control finances are a symptom of an out of control life." Turn a new leaf on your financial life by asking Jesus Christ to fill that great big empty hole inside of you with His Holy Spirit. When you do, you will find money will resume its proper place in your life: as a servant, not a master. It will be the start of a harmonious financial life in your marriage.

QUESTIONS FOR SMALL GROUP DISCUSSION

1. The Gallup poll statistic is that 64% of all couples argue over money. Do you think that number is an accurate reflection or is it too high or too low? Do you know any couples who fight over money?

2. Financial disagreements can cause intense stress in a marriage. What issues contribute to financial tension between couples?

3. Why is keeping good records so important to staying out of financial troubles?

4. Discuss impulse buying. Tell of one time when you bought something on impulse and later regretted it. Then, tell of one time when you didn't buy on the impulse and later were glad you hadn't.

5. Discuss the various ways that a couple can effectively budget their money. If you have a system that works for you, share it with the group.

6. Have you every considered burying your (or your spouse's) credit card in cement?

7. Why is saving money so difficult to do for many of us?

8. What is your opinion of gambling?

9. One of the most controversial areas today is that of money and the church. What is your opinion of tithing?

10. What, in your opinion, are the keys to contentment?

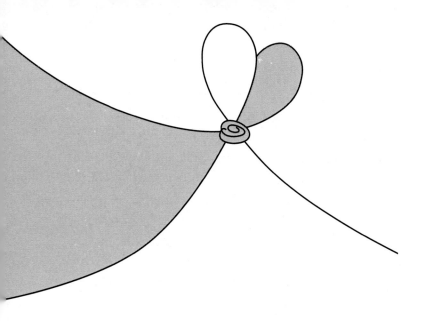

FIGHT THE GOOD FIGHT

A fellow was asked if he and his wife had ever fought. "No," he said. "But we *have* had discussions that you could hear three blocks away!" Conflict is inevitable and every marriage goes through times when couples disagree—even a pastor and his wife. Like the cartoon in which the pastor's wife is saying to her husband, "I know the Lord loves you. It's just that sometimes I wonder why."

There are many things pulling couples and families apart today, including the fast pace of life we live and the resulting stress we place ourselves under. Then there is the very negative influence of our society, particularly that of the media: the TV programs we watch, the movies we go to, the magazines and books we read, the internet sites we visit. I believe we are experiencing a massive brainwashing of our society by the media today. Add to that our own sinful human nature with its natural tendency to self-centeredness and the result is that many families are experiencing conflict. In this chapter, we will take a look at some practical steps, right out of God's word, to resolve conflict; instead of being pulled apart, we can pull together.[55]

Jesus knew the negative impact that conflict makes on a home: "Jesus knew their thoughts and said to them, 'Every...household divided against itself will not stand'" (Matthew 12:25). We can work against that destructive factor by doing what Paul instructs to do in all of the Christian life: "Fight the good fight..." (1 Timothy 6:12).

THE REASON FOR CONFLICT

The Bible is very blunt when it comes to the reason for conflict. It clearly points out selfishness as the root cause.

> What causes fights and quarrels among you? Don't they come from your desires that battle within you? You want something but don't get it. You kill and covet, but you cannot have what you want. You quarrel and fight.
>
> James 4:1–2

I want what I want because at the core of my being,

I am basically a selfish person. I think of me before I think of you (and you do too!). When those competing desires collide, that is called conflict.

Selfishness comes from the fact that we are all sinful human beings. The Bible says, "For all have sinned and fall short of the glory of God" (Romans 3:23). When Adam and Eve disobeyed God and took of the fruit, the curse placed upon them was that of a sinful human nature: "Therefore, just as sin entered the world through one man, and death through sin, and in this way death came to all men, because all sinned" (Romans 5:12). You got your sinful nature from your father and he got it from his father and so on, all the way back to Adam. As a result of this sinful nature, conflict to some degree is inevitable in every family.

Columnist Anne Landers once received a letter from a man who called himself "Embattled in Elmhurst." In it, he complained, "Right hand to God, this is no joke. I am both mystified and burned up. Please give me your opinion. I can't go to anyone else. I am 58 years old, married to a good woman for 34 years. Our marriage is no better, no worse than most others. She's not perfect but then, neither am I. The problem: I'm a heavy sleeper, and I snore. My wife says my snoring has really gotten bad this past year, and it interferes with her rest."

"Last night, she gave me a headband with a bicycle horn attached to it. The horn is in the back. When the snorer turns to sleep on his back, the horn blows and wakes him up. I tried the blame thing on and it was very uncomfortable. Also, the horn is loud and it would scare me out of my wits if I blew it during the night. I refused to wear it. Do you feel I am justified?" Landers replied, "You're darned tootin'!"

But God is most concerned about how you handle conflict. The best God-honoring way is when we care about the relationship more than any single issue we have with each other. I not only care about solving the problem, but I care about the relationship and I care about you. This is the attitude the Apostle Paul enjoins upon us, when he says,

> Make my joy complete by being like-minded, having the same love, being one in spirit and purpose. Do nothing out of selfish ambition or vain conceit, but in humility consider others better than yourselves. Each of you should look not only to your own interests, but also to the interests of others.
>
> Philippians 2:24

As believers in Jesus, we value our relationship more than the things we tend to fight over. I want us to have a mutually satisfactory resolution to this conflict because you are important and our relationship is important.

THE RESOLUTION TO CONFLICT

How do we have such a relationship? How do we solve our conflicts? Let me share some steps we all need to take:

PRAY TO GOD FOR HELP

Before you can call on God for help, you need to become a Christian. That is the starting point. Believe that Jesus died on the cross, and accept Him as your personal Savior. You cannot have peace with other people until you first have peace with God. Before I became a Christian, according to the Bible, I was in conflict with Him. "For if, when we were God's enemies, we were reconciled to him through the death of his Son..." (Romans 5:10). When I am having conflict with God vertically, it spills out horizontally to all my other relationships.

Many marriage problems would be solved if husbands and wives would simply give themselves to Jesus Christ. Then there would be harmony and unity in those same marriages now being devastated by conflict. The scriptures say,

> For he himself is our peace, who has made the two one and has destroyed the barrier, the dividing wall of hostility, by abolishing in his flesh the law with its commandments and regulations. His purpose was to create in himself one new man out of the two, thus making peace, and in this one body to reconcile both of them to God through the cross, by which he put to death their hostility.
>
> Ephesians 2:14–16

So, I urge you, please open your heart up to Jesus Christ today and become a believer. This is what happened to Tom and Nancy (names changed to protect identity), a couple in our church. Their marriage had been fraught with all sorts of difficulties and conflicts, primarily because of Tom's excessive drinking. Then, while on a trip, Tom realized his desperate need and prayed with a pastor friend to accept Christ. The change was immediate. When he returned home, Nancy immediately saw the change in Tom, especially when he poured his alcohol down the drain. Subsequently, she too prayed to receive Christ. Today, 35 years later, their marriage survives and thrives because of that step.

Secondly, pray about it. In the passage we looked at earlier from James 4, speaking of conflict, James says, "You want something but don't get it. You kill and covet, but you cannot have what you want. You quarrel and fight. You do not have, because you do not ask God" (James 4:2). The Message translates it like this:

> Where do you think all these appalling wars and quarrels come from? Do you think they just happen? Think again. They come about because you want your own way, and fight for it deep inside yourselves. You lust for what you don't have and are willing to kill to get it. You want what isn't yours and will risk violence to get your hands on it. You wouldn't think of just asking God for it, would you?

I like the way it says, "You wouldn't think of just asking God for it, would you?" Conflict often occurs when we are looking to our spouse, or to other people, to meet the needs that only God Himself can meet in our lives.

We make that person god and when we do, we set ourselves up for huge disappointment and bitterness.

One day you stood at the front of a church and you said, "I do." Perhaps you did not realize it then but what you were really saying was, "I expect." It is likely you were not thinking at all about your responsibilities in the marriage relationship. Rather, you were thinking how, now, all your needs would be met by this person. But let me say this as clearly as I can—there is no human being on earth who can possibly meet *all* your needs. No one. Only God can do that. My former associate pastor, Howard Moore, once made the statement, "The greatest reason for marital problems and divorce is unmet expectations." I totally agree.

What are the indicators that show me I am expecting my spouse to meet those deep, deep needs that God alone can? It is when I find myself getting angry at the other person. Anger is a signal to us which says "I am looking to you to meet my needs!" For example, when my need is for you to affirm my worth as a person, and when, for whatever reason, you do not, I get angry. That indicates I am looking to you to meet those basic needs, and because you are not doing it for me, I become upset.

But scripture says, "You have not because you do not ask God." Instead of expecting our mate to meet all our needs, God wants us to look to Him. The classic hymn, "What a friend we have in Jesus" says, "Oh, what needless pain we bear all because we do not take it to the Lord in prayer."

The correct first step is to discuss it with God. When you do, you may find that this will solve the problem right then and there. "I sought the Lord, and he answered me; he delivered me from all my fears...This poor man called, and the Lord heard him; he saved him out of all his troubles" (Psalm 34:4–6).

Many times, I have had things bothering me in my life that were a source of major irritation for me. Every time that I went to God in prayer, in one way or another, He would bring an answer to that very thing that had been bothering me. I heard one pastor say that had been true in his relationship with his wife. He said, "When I have been irritated with her about some issue or there had been some conflict in our relationship, I would go to God and pray about it first. The result was that God would either change my heart, or sometimes, He would change her heart without me even having to talk about it."

There are so many things that could be smoother in your marriage if you would just pray about it first.

ADMIT TO YOUR PART IN THE CONFLICT

Ask yourself: "How much of this is my fault?" Everyone has blind spots. "Why do you look at the speck of sawdust in your brother's eye and pay no attention to the plank in your own eye?" (Matthew 7:3). Now this is one of the funniest verses in the Bible, one which when Jesus spoke it to His audience of first century Jews, it would have had everyone laughing. That is because Hebrew humor often uses hyperbole. Hyperbole is exaggeration for effect. We use hyperbole when we say, "I'm so hungry I could eat a horse!" or "I told you a million times to not exaggerate!"

So, when Jesus says, "Before you start getting the sawdust speck out of your partner's eye, why don't you get the log out of yours?" He is using exaggeration to say, "Check yourself out first. Look at your own self." We all have blind spots because nobody is perfect. So I need to ask: "Am I the problem? Am I being unrealistic? Am I being insensitive? Am I being overly sensitive? Am I being too demanding? Am I being ungrateful?"

The first step in dealing with conflict is to look at yourself and ask yourself what problems am I bringing into the relationship? Ogden Nash gave this advice: "To keep your marriage brimming with love in the loving cup, when you're wrong admit it. And when you're right, shut up!"

Many people use, as an excuse for divorce, the statement: "We're just incompatible." That statement has such an innocent, "no fault" air to it. But listen to what three of the leading experts on marriage have to say about the issue of incompatibility. Dr. Paul Tournier, the Swiss psychiatrist who wrote *To Understand Each Other,* says, "So called incompatibility is a myth invented by jurists in order to plead for divorce. It is likewise a common excuse for people to hide their own weaknesses and failings. Misunderstandings and mistakes can be corrected when there is a willingness to do so. The problem is the lack of complete frankness."[56]

Paul Popineau, Director of the Institute of Family Relations, says, "I don't believe in incompatibility. I don't believe it exists. Almost any two people are compatible if they try to be." [57] Dr. Archibald Hart comments, "If people can be divorced for incompatibility, I cannot conceive why all of us are not divorced."[58]

Actually, fundamental "incompatibility" is a given in marriage. "I have known many happy marriages," G. K. Chesterton once said, "but never a compatible one."[59] As I quoted Odgen Nash at the beginning of the book, "So I hope husbands and wives will continue to debate and combat over everything debatable and combatable,/ Because I believe a little incompatibility is the spice of life, particularly if he has income and she is pattable."

"If we say we are without sin we deceive ourselves and the truth is not in us" (1 John 1:8). You and I each have an infinite capacity for self deception. The easiest thing in the world for me to do is to blame you for all my problems. The reality is that it is not incompatibility that is the problem. The root problem is really selfishness and an unwillingness to change. When marriages come to an end, it is because either one, or both, is selfish and unwilling to change. And the fact of the matter is that you will carry that selfishness and unwillingness to change into the next relationship whatever it might be.

So, begin by admitting to your part in the conflict.

HAVE A PEACE CONFERENCE

Third, determine to have a meeting in which you and your spouse intentionally set about to deal with the conflict. Conflict is seldom settled accidentally—it must be done intentionally because it does not resolve itself. As a matter a fact, conflict worsens when you avoid the issue. As time progresses, people's hearts grow harder and their positions get solidified. Walls are erected instead of bridges. So you have to intentionally deal with the conflict. That is why Jesus says in Matthew 5:23–24, "Therefore, if you are offering your gift at the altar and there remember that your brother has something against you, leave your gift there in front of the altar. First go and be reconciled to your brother; then come and offer your gift." What Jesus is saying is that it is impossible to worship God when you have unresolved issues with others. 1 John 4:20 says, "If anyone says, 'I love God,' yet hates his brother, he is a liar. For anyone who does not love his brother, whom he has seen, cannot love God, whom he has not seen."

That is why Satan loves to try to get you into a conflict before you get to church. Do you ever have conflicts in your car on your way to church? That is his favorite time to get you into a fight. Linda and I solved that problem long ago. We go to church in separate cars so we do not have conflicts coming to church any more. (Actually, as the pastor, I arrive at church very early on Sunday mornings and she comes later in her own car!)

But Jesus is saying you cannot worship God with

conflict in your heart. 1 Peter 3:7 goes as far as to say that disharmony with your spouse will hinder your prayers. You may be wondering, "How come God is not answering my prayers?" Maybe it's because you need to get something right with your husband or wife first.

Jesus says don't ignore it. If you are in the act of worshipping God, and it is then that you remember your brother has something against you (usually it is when I am attempting to worship God that He reminds me of my sins anyway), go and deal with the issue. And really, it does not matter if you are the offended person or if you are the offender. Either way, Jesus is saying "Go to that person. The ball is in your court." And when do you do it? Immediately. Jesus says, "Leave your gift at that altar." Do not say, "I'll do it later." Postponed conflict only gets worse. Ephesians 4:26 tells us, "Do not let the sun go down while you are still angry." That means that you do it in that very same day. The longer you leave conflict unresolved, the longer it festers and subsequently, turns into bitterness. That is why you need to do it as soon as possible.

Rick Warren gives three practical suggestions about having a peace conference. The first is to choose the right time. It is very important to have this meeting at the right time. Timing is of ultimate importance when you are trying to resolve conflict. I would suggest that late at night is definitely not the right time. I know that for me, things always look worse at the end of the day, when I am tired. The same problem in the morning always looks smaller. It is for that reason you should not try to resolve conflict in bed. Let me tell you why. Here is the wife who has been stewing about the problem all day. She thinks she has finally figured out what is wrong with the marriage. So, husband and wife get into bed, and she begins to explain her side of the story. On the other side of the bed is a husband growing drowsier and drowsier by the minute. As she comes to what she thinks is the solution to the problem, she hears snoring. Now that tends to put a definite chill into the air. The problem now is ten times worse because she is mad at him for the original problem *and* for not listening and going to sleep. But the truth of the matter is that any man in the prone position will be sawing logs before ten minutes are up. That is simply the way they are made. Do not try to do a peace conference in bed. When is the best time to have a peace conference? The best time is when you are both at your best, when you are not tired, not hurried, not rushed.

Second, he says, choose the right place. A husband was asked the secret of his long healthy life and many years of marriage. He told of the deal they made on their wedding day. "If I was unhappy with her, she would go into another room. If she was unhappy with me, then I'd go outside." He concluded, "I spent most of my life outdoors." You need to find a place where you can be alone, uninterrupted, where the kids are not running through the house. Take the phone off the hook so that you are uninterrupted.

Third, he recommends, pray before the meeting. Your marriage may be on the edge of divorce right now, but I would suggest that before you have the conference, you sit down, hold hands and pray. Ask God to give you wisdom in the peace conference so that you will not say the right thing in the wrong way and be misunderstood.

But, as I have said, let it be you who takes the initiative. Jesus tells us to go to the other person. So, you be the mature one in the relationship and take the initiative to convene a peace conference.

WATCH YOUR LANGUAGE

Ephesians 4:29 says, "Do not let any unwholesome talk come out of your mouths, but only what is helpful for building others up according to their needs, that it may benefit those who listen." We need to be very careful about the words we use when we are dealing with conflict. We need to eliminate all inflammatory words and threats. The Bible says we are to communicate in love (Ephesians 4:15). Otherwise we can do more harm than good.

During the Cold War, the West and the Soviet Union had an agreement they called the Strategic Arms Reduction Treaty. Part of that treaty was an agreement to not use certain weapons. For example, nuclear arms were out of bounds. Even though they were fighting a battle, they agreed that some weapons were too devastating to be used.

The Bible is very specific about what you are not to use in a conflict. Colossians 3:8 in J.B. Philips' translation, The New Testament in Modern English, says, "You must put away all these things—furious rage, malice, insults, and shouted abuse. Don't deceive each other with lies anymore." In this list, note that Paul says five things are out of bounds:

1. "*Furious rage.*" Rage is always a conflict resolution stopper; in fact, it creates even more problems. Some people use rage as a means of controlling and getting their own way. One man I know would blow up to frighten everyone into doing his wishes. It worked.

2. "*Malice.*" Malice is saying things to intentionally hurt, wound, or destroy.

3. "*Insults.*" Insulting statements include belittling, labeling, judging or put down remarks. Someone has said, "Little men belittle their wives."

4. "*Shouted abuse.*" Shouting abuse at your spouse is out of bounds. In over 35 years of marriage, I have never yelled at Linda. That's because when we were getting married, she chose a bulletin cover that had, on the back of it, 10 *Steps to a Happy Marriage*. I still remember number seven: "Never yell, except when the house is on fire!" The house has never caught fire so I haven't had to do it.

5. "*Don't deceive each other with lies.*" Tell the truth. We lie when we use the phrases "always" and "never." For example, when you say, "You always...," that is simply not true. When you say to me, "You always...,"

I then mentally try to think up of one time when I didn't do it that way. And usually, I am successful in coming up with more than one illustration to justify myself. The same thing can also be said about the phrase, "You never..." So, eliminate the "always" and the "nevers."

The point of telling the truth is to say what you mean. At the same time, do not use side issues. If you do not like the way your husband is not paying attention to you, do not criticize the way he drives. Deal with the issue that is troubling you, not something else. If you are bothered about your sexual relationship, don't argue about the lawn not being mowed.

Do not play mind reader. This is a favorite game among marriage partners. "You know..." No, I do not. "You know what I am upset about." No, I do not. "If you loved me, you would know!" Say what you mean, and be clear and accurate. Rick Warren says, "You never get your point across by being cross. And you're never persuasive when you're abrasive. You have to learn how to argue without assassinating. You have to learn to speak the truth in love."[60]

You may need to go to your spouse today and ask forgiveness from them for the way you have been talking to them. You may have to say, "From now on, no matter how angry we are at each other, we are going to speak the truth in love." "Instead, speaking the truth in love, we will in all things grow up into him who is the Head, that is, Christ" (Ephesians 4:15).

LOOK AT IT FROM YOUR SPOUSE'S PERSPECTIVE

From our own perspective, we are always in the right. "Every way of a man is right in his own eyes" (Proverbs 21:2, KJV). As result, that becomes one of the causes of conflict: seeing things only from our own perspective. To resolve conflict, you need to decide to not just look at things from your own viewpoint, but to also look at them from your spouse's viewpoint. Now, for most of us this is very difficult. It is not natural for me to look at life from Linda's viewpoint. It requires an intentional shift where I change the focus from looking at my needs to looking at her needs. It is not easy, and we do not do it naturally. But it is the secret of resolving conflict.

One of the secrets to resolving conflict is to understand where people are coming from. The better you understand somebody, the less conflict you are likely to have with them. So, how do you learn to understand them? Listen to them. Listen more than you talk. This, again, is not easy for many of us. It certainly is not easy for me. My natural ability is to talk. Sometimes, I get so anxious to make my point that I do not even listen to what Linda is saying. As she is talking, I am already planning what I am going to say back to her. I need to heed what St. Francis of Assisi prayed, "O Divine Master, grant that I may not so much seek to be consoled as to console; to be understood as to understand..."[61] and do it myself.

There are two particular areas in a marriage that you need to be considerate of. Romans 15:2 in the Living

Bible tells us, "We must bear the burden of being considerate of the doubts and fears of others." The reason we are to be considerate of the doubts and fears of others is because they look so silly to us. My doubts and my fears are all reasonable, logical, and make perfectly good sense, but your fears are irrational, illogical and stupid.

The Bible says, "Each of you should look not only to your own interests, but also to the interests of others. Your attitude should be the same as that of Christ Jesus" (Philippians 2:4). You are most like Jesus when you ask, "What are her/his needs and how can I meet them?" Typically, we are preoccupied with ourselves. But when we are like Christ, we look to each other's interest and not merely our own.

One of the most powerful peace making statements is when you say to your husband/wife, "I am sorry. I was only thinking of myself." Likely, when you say that, it will cause them to faint. But when they wake up from it, you can probably then get started on the road to recovery in the relationship.

CONCLUSION

Conflict in a marriage can really wear you down. It can get you to the place where you want to simply throw in the towel and give up. However, my counsel is don't do it! Realize that it is more rewarding to resolve a conflict than it is to dissolve a relationship. So, here are a couple of practical suggestions:

BE WILLING TO GET GOOD CHRISTIAN COUNSELING

When you have a medical problem in your body, you are not ashamed to go to the doctor. On a recent trip home from Israel, my back was causing me incredible pain from being on planes and in airports for 60 straight hours. When I got home, I did not hesitate to go see my chiropractor. After a short session with him manipulating my back, most of the pain, thankfully, was gone. I did not feel embarrassed by that. When I was having a problem with my high golf scores, I was not ashamed of going to a golf pro and getting some advice on how to improve my game.

In the same way, when you have a relational problem, there is nothing wrong with getting someone who is a relational professional, someone who knows more than you do about how relationships work. That is where good Christian counseling comes in. I am convinced that many marriages could have been saved from divorce if they would have just gotten some help. Many marriages are miserable, and they go year after with the same old problems, because they are just too proud to go get help.

Rick Warren, pastor of Saddleback Church in California says, "Most of you know that when Kay and I were having those bad early years, we went to a marriage counselor. I was making $800 a month and the counseling was $100 a week. I racked up a $1500 bill on my MasterCard. I've often said I should do a commercial: 'MasterCard saved my marriage!' I look back now and ask, 'Was it worth it?' That was the best $1500

I ever spent. It saved my marriage and saved my happiness. I'd pay a million bucks for it today. I'd pay two million dollars for what I have today."

He goes on to say, "When people say, 'We can't afford counseling', I say, 'You can't afford not to get it.' If your marriage is in shambles, what are you willing to pay to save it? What are you willing to do to keep a stable home for your kids? If you have to take out a loan, do it. It's far better than taking out a loan on a car and you do that all the time. A car is going to die after seven or eight years. If it took you 25 years to pay it off but it saved your marriage, it would be worth it. There are a lot of kids out there, with many fears; many hurts, just waiting for mom and dad to reconcile."[62]

GET GOD'S HELP

Finally, recognize that you cannot do this on your own and that you need God's power and help to put your marriage back together again. Many marriage conflicts would be solved overnight if both the husband and the wife would kneel before God and say to Him, "We humble ourselves before You and ask You to make our marriage work. We submit our egos and our hurts to You. Jesus Christ, do what only You can do." As someone has put it, "Christ is the only third party in a marriage who can make it work."

"Blessed are the peacemakers for they will be called sons of God" (Matthew 5:9).

QUESTIONS FOR SMALL GROUP DISCUSSION

1. "Conflict is inevitable and every marriage goes through times when couples disagree." Without causing a fight, tell of some conflicts you have had that you later successfully resolved.

2. Analyze the Bible's claim that conflict's roots are always in selfishness. Can you see evidences of selfishness in yourself that has caused conflict in some of your relationships in the past?

3. Discuss each of the steps suggested to solve conflict in marriage:

   a) Pray to God for help—Why is this so crucial?

   b) Admit your part in the conflict—How will this help?

   c) Have a peace conference—Tell of a peace conference you have attempted in your past.

   d) Watch your language—What are some struggles you face in this area?

   e) Look at it from your mate's perspective—Tell what happens when you do.

4. Why are many people fearful of or unwilling to go to Christian counseling?

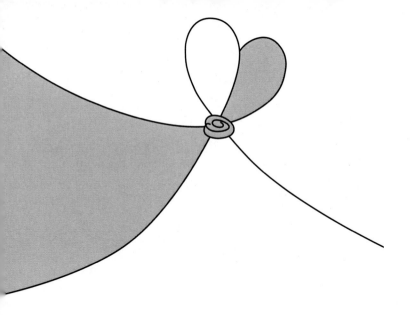

A MARRIAGE MAKEOVER

A "Husband Shopping Centre" was opened where women could go to choose, from among many men, a husband. It was laid out in five floors. The only rule was that, once you opened the door to any floor, you had to choose a man from that floor. If you went up a floor, you could not go back down except to leave the place.

So, a couple of women went to find a man. On the first floor, they saw a sign saying: "These men have jobs and love kids." The women read the sign and said, "Well, that's better than not having jobs and not loving kids, but what's further up?" So up they went.

The sign on the second floor said, "These men have high paying jobs, love kids and are extremely good looking." "Hmmm..." wondered the women, "But what's further up?"

The sign on the third floor said, "These men have high paying jobs, love kids, are extremely good looking and help with the housework." "Wow!" said the women, "Very tempting but there's more further up!" And so they went up further.

On the fourth floor, the sign read, "These men have high paying jobs, love kids, are extremely good looking, help with the housework and have a strong romantic streak." "Oh, mercy me!" said the women. "But just think. What must be awaiting us on the fifth floor?"

The sign on the fifth floor said, "This floor is just to prove that women are impossible to please. Thank you for shopping and have a nice day!"

Well, finding the perfect husband (or wife) may be impossible. I remember talking to a bachelor in my congregation. I asked him why he never married. "I guess it's because I was looking for the perfect woman..." he said. "And you never found her?" I further questioned him. "No," he replied, "I did." He sighed, "But just my luck, she was looking for the perfect man!"

All of us have married imperfect people, which in turn sometimes leads to us being not happy in our marriage. What do you do? Some marriages might benefit by what I am calling "a marriage makeover." On The Learning Channel, some time ago, I watched a program called *A Makeover Story*. In it, two people get a full makeover treatment from the experts. They go through a complete transformation that includes hair, makeup, and wardrobe. The changes are quite amazing. In this chapter, we will take a look at how to transform a marriage: the ABCDE of a marriage makeover.[63]

A - ACCEPT RESPONSIBILITY FOR MY PART IN THE MARRIAGE

We cannot control our spouse's actions and attitudes, but we can control our own. We can be responsible for our part of the problem and for our part of the solution. That means we have to stop blaming our spouse for our unhappiness. Our ultimate happiness is not determined by him or by her. We are as happy as we choose to be.

You also have to stop complaining about your marriage, having a pity party. A woman complained to her friend, "My husband and I are getting along together fairly well, but he simply can't bear children." "Oh well," her friend consoled her, "you can't expect men to do everything."

When we come to the place where we accept responsibility for our marriage, we will also stop daydreaming about being married to someone else. Fantasies like: "Why couldn't I be married to someone like Tom Cruise?" or "I wonder what it'd be like being hitched up to Katie Holmes" will have to go. The reason people fantasize about being married to someone else is because they think the grass is greener on the other side of the fence. I like the way one pastor put it: "The grass is not greener on the other side of the fence and the grass is not greener on this side of the fence. The grass is greener where you water it, where you put forth the effort."

If you want to have a magnificent marriage, stop fantasizing, daydreaming, complaining, and blaming. Take all that same energy and start watering and weeding. Then watch what happens. Start working on your marriage by assuming responsibility. "Each person must be responsible for himself" (Galatians 6:5, NCV).

B - BELIEVE YOUR MARRIAGE CAN CHANGE

Some people reach the place where they begin to feel their marriage is hopeless. You may be feeling that way. You may be thinking, "It's past the point of no return!" You feel like giving up. You may feel your marriage is on the rocks; you may feel it is hopeless. From a human standpoint, your marriage may be on its last leg, in the coffin and nailing the lid down, the heart monitor beep is going slower and slower. But let me say this: from God's viewpoint, nothing is impossible for the marriage where two people have faith in God. God has not given up. The Bible says, "Humanly speaking, it is impossible. But with God, everything is possible!" (Matthew 19:26, NLT).

You may be saying things like: "But you don't know my marriage. You don't know how much I've been hurt. You don't know the things we've said to each other in our marriage. You don't know what's gone on and the unfaithfulness and the other things." It is true that I do not know your marriage, but I *do* know that nothing is impossible with God! No matter how bad your situation, give it to God. The Bible says, "For God is working in you, giving you the desire to obey him and the power to do what pleases him" (Philippians 2:13, NLT).

One of the great joys of my ministry has been to remarry people whose marriages had failed, and they divorced. Then, through the intervention of God through faith, they reconciled and subsequently asked me to remarry them. One of those was after the couple had been divorced from each other for 15 years. That is always a fun occasion, let me assure you.

But, I urge you, believe your marriage can change.

C - COMMIT TO DOING WHATEVER IT TAKES

It takes hard work to make a great marriage. Great marriages do not just happen—they take effort. "Don't get tired of doing what is good. Don't get discouraged and give up" (Galatians 6:9, NLT). It also takes humility—a willingness to say, "I was wrong. Please forgive me." A lot of people aren't willing to do that. My response is to say that "proud people's marriages end." "All of you, clothe yourselves with humility toward one another, because, 'God opposes the proud but gives grace to the humble'" (I Peter 5:5).

Third, it takes time. You did not get into this mess overnight, and you will not get out of it overnight. Did you hear about the Amish man who married an Amish woman? Within a week, he'd driven her buggy! In the same way, it will take time to get your marriage going again, but you *will* be able to do it.

Unfortunately, many people are not willing to do the hard work. It is so much easier to throw in the towel and divorce. Some people give up too soon. They check out, go find somebody new, and never do deal with the issues. The problem is that when you go into that new relationship, you take you along. And you are half the problem and those issues are still unresolved. As my friend Wally says, "My problem is that wherever I go, I go too and spoil everything!" It has been statistically proven that more people divorce in their second marriage and even more in their third.

Make the commitment to do whatever it takes, to pay the price that is needed to be paid.

D - DEAL WITH UNRESOLVED HURTS

Begin by asking for forgiveness for what you have done that is wrong. The Bible teaches, "Admit your faults to one another" (James 5:16, LB). Say to your spouse, "I am sorry. I was only thinking of myself." (Now, there is an admission that not only is out of the ordinary but also has a tremendously powerful effect on transforming a marriage. It is humbling but works wonders).

Then, offer forgiveness to your spouse for hurting you. The Bible says, "Be gentle and ready to forgive; never hold grudges. Remember, the Lord forgave you, so you must forgive others" (Colossians 3:13, TLB). I am convinced that if every couple did this, divorce and broken homes would drop by 90%. I know you may have been really hurt by him/her, but remember, you can forgive. God will never ask you to forgive more than what He has already forgiven you.

E - ENLIST SUPPORT FROM OTHERS

Finally, you will need support that helps you stay together as a couple. Today, everything in our culture works against marriage and staying together. Many people will tell you: "If you're not happy, leave!" But you need godly advice from someone who is spiritually mature and knows God's Word. The Bible says, "Get all the advice and instruction you can, and be wise the rest of your life" (Proverbs 19:20, NLT). Be careful whom you go to for counsel; make sure it is someone who clearly knows and understands God's word. "Blessed is the man who does not walk in the counsel of the wicked...But his delight is in the law of the Lord, and on his law he meditates day and night" (Psalm 1:1–2). This support will help you to stay together. "It takes wisdom to have a good family and it takes understanding to make it strong" (Proverbs 24:3, NCV).

As I said before, couples having marital struggles are frequently given the advice: "if you're not happy, leave." Let me respond to that advice by saying this: God is more interested in our holiness than He is in our happiness. The Bible tells us to "make every effort to live in peace with all men and to be holy; without holiness no one will see the Lord." In God's order of priorities for your life, your holiness is a lot higher than your happiness. A commitment to holiness may mean making a commitment to stay and work through marriage problems even if you are unhappy. In today's culture, I recognize how heretical that sounds, but you do that because you know God cares more about your holiness and you fulfilling His will in your life than anything else. Once you reach the level of holiness God wants in your life, you will be amazed at the happiness you will experience. He may even give you the amazing marriage you long for.

CONCLUSION

Perhaps you are saying, "I would love for my marriage to work. I do not want it to be what it is. But I am so tired of trying. I have tried for years to make this thing work, and I feel like I am batting my head against a brick wall. I am out of energy, and I am ready to give up. I am powerless to change my marriage." Let me assure you that God can give you the power to do what needs to be done to make your marriage work. "For I can do everything with the help of Christ who gives me the strength I need" (Philippians 4:13, NLT).

I am so convinced of this, that I will offer a "money back guarantee" (that is, if you paid for this book): if both of you, as husband and wife, will carefully and faithfully follow the ABCDE of a marriage makeover, your marriage *will* be saved and you will truly be happy in it. But only if *both of you* are willing and do follow through on what the Scriptures teach.

Some of my earliest memories of childhood are that of my parents fighting. I remember sitting by the upstairs heating grate that enabled me to listen in on their conversations downstairs and just hating it. Their quarreling made me feel so insecure. Then, when I was about six, they both turned to God. He did a marriage makeover for them that lasted. When my mom died in 2001, they had been married 67 years. What God did for them, He can also do for you.

QUESTIONS FOR SMALL GROUP DISCUSSION

1. As you begin, do you believe it is realistic to think that people can honestly have a "marriage makeover"? Or is it a "pipe dream" for most couples? Why or why not?

2. The majority of people have fantasized about being married to someone else other than their present partner. How can this affect a marriage? What are some Biblical truths to help you control your mind?

3. Discuss the statement: "The grass is not greener on the other side of the fence and it is not greener on this side of the fence. The grass is greener where

you water it." Why are we inclined to look "on the other side?" How can we "water the grass" where we are?

4. Why is believing your marriage can change so important? Can God do the impossible? Why does it not always happen? What holds it back?

5. It is hard work to have a great marriage. Why are people so often unwilling to do that hard work?

6. Give some reasons why asking your spouse for forgiveness for your wrongs and forgiving your spouse for theirs has such a powerful transforming effect on a marriage.

7. Why is having the support of others such a help in renewing one's marriage? Why do couples without it tend to have greater struggles?

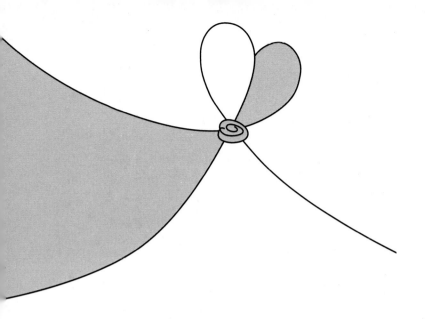

TILL DIVORCE PARTS US

One of my dad's favorite magazines used to be the *National Enquirer*. "They have such interesting news, compared to regular papers!" he would say. Some time ago, I picked up an edition of the *Enquirer* that had an article by John Blosser entitled, "Wacky Things Stars Said Before Marriage–And AFTER Divorce," I found it fascinating. For example, did you know that Marilyn Monroe, speaking about her second husband, Joe DiMaggio, said, "A man's career is wonderful and exciting." She said that before her divorce from him. But after the divorce, she said: "All he did was watch cowboys on television." Richard Burton spoke about Elizabeth Taylor, before they were married: "Elizabeth's body is a miracle of construction, and a work of an engineer of genius." After the divorce, he said: "She is too fat and her legs are too short." Bridgette Bardot said of her second husband, actor Jacques Charier, before marriage: "I love him so much. His pain is my pain." (He was suffering from appendicitis at the time.) After the divorce, she said: "He was such a problem." Rita Hayworth promised before marrying her fourth husband, Dick Haymes: "I will follow him anywhere in the world." After they split up, she said: "I don't know where he is, and I don't care." Zsa Zsa Gabor gushed about her second husband, George Sanders, before their marriage: "I am so in love with him!" After it was over, she complained: "The trouble is we were both in love with him."[64]

Cully Olson, a traveling evangelist who spoke in our church, had this comment about Hollywood actresses: "All of them are such good housekeepers. After this divorce, they get to keep this house; after that divorce, they get to keep that house..." Did you hear about the Hollywood couple who got divorced and then got remarried? The divorce didn't work out! Lewis Grizzard once said, "Instead of getting married again, I'm just gonna find a woman I don't like and give her a house!" They say there's a new Barbie doll out. It's called "Divorce Barbie." She comes with all of Ken's stuff.

But, really, divorce is not a laughing matter. It is a tragedy and one of the biggest problems facing our society today. It has taken on epidemic proportions. Canada, for example, has one of the highest divorce rates in the industrialized world. One recently released study says that overall, about one-third of all marriages in Canada end in divorce and the rate is somewhat higher for remarriages. Dissolution rates are even higher among cohabiting couples.

So, in this chapter, we will look, from a Biblical perspective, at this tragic topic. Though this is a big topic, I will try to keep it brief and to the point. Just like Elizabeth Taylor says to all her husbands: "I won't keep you long!"

THE HIGH COST OF DIVORCE

Diane Medvid, a clinical psychologist in Santa Monica, California, writes, "Divorce is so disastrous to body, mind, and spirit that in an overwhelming number of cases, the cure of divorce is worse than the disease."[65] Gary Richmond, writing in an article entitled, "When Families Break Up: The Human Toll," comments, "Divorce spawns far more problems than it solves."[66]

It is because of the high cost of divorce that God in scripture says, "I hate divorce" (Malachi 2:16). He hates it because it costs people dearly. There are at least three costs that come with divorce.

COST ON THE CHILDREN

First of all, there is the cost on the children. Perhaps you heard of the couple who went to the divorce lawyer at the age of 90, after 70 years of marriage and asked for a divorce. He was perplexed and asked, "Why did you wait till 90 to divorce?" She replied, "We wanted to wait till the children died." Then there's the lady who confided to her friend, "We're only staying together because of the children. Neither of us wants them!"

After 30 to 40 years of unrestrained divorcing in our society, research has now brought the verdict in: in a divorce, children definitely are the losers. They used to say, "It doesn't affect children." We now know how wrong that statement is. Research has shown that children of divorce are 40 percent to 75 percent more likely to repeat a grade and 70 percent more likely to be expelled from school. Children who grow up in fractured families are less likely to graduate from high school than children from intact families. A disproportionate number of runaway teens come from step-parent households. Young sons often experience nightmares and a "father hunger" soon after the dad leaves home. In their teens, they are more likely to have increased levels of aggression, gang membership and other emotional and behavioral problems. Young daughters of divorce often experience anxiety and guilt. In their teens, they are more likely to be sexually involved, marry younger, be pregnant more often before marriage, and become divorced or separated from their eventual husbands. Children of divorce typically experience depression, drug and alcohol experimentation and a diminishing ability to form lasting relationships.[67]

Children of divorce experience more illness, both mental and physical. A disproportionate number of runaway teens come from divorced households. They are often subjected to the repeated tugging of two parents fighting for their time and emotional support. They are frequently forced into taking sides, even though that is the last thing in the world that they want to do.[68]

Recently, a father named Bob told his pastor how his marriage was steadily deteriorating. He no longer slept in the same bedroom with his wife. During an intense fight, Bob would leave the house rather than stay and be berated in front of the children. Sharon, his wife, would fall into depression. She would sit for hours doing needlepoint or reading the same page of the newspaper, over and over again. The two youngest children were left to fend for themselves. Cold cereal and quick snacks were their diet. One night, Bob heard his five-year-old daughter, Julie, quietly call him. He stuck his head into her bedroom and gruffly asked, "What are you doing up?" Julie reached up her arms and whispered, "Daddy, will you hold me?" Bob pulled her close and listened. "Daddy," she said in a quivering voice, "it's just that I don't know if anyone loves me anymore."

Recently, Linda was on a flight, sitting next to a gentleman who was in his 80's. As they spoke, he told her how he was moving some 1300 miles from Thunder Bay, Ontario to Edmonton, Alberta to live closer to his daughter. The conversation moved to the topic of divorce and its pain. He said to Linda, "I understand it completely. My parents divorced when I was a young boy, and I still feel the pain."

THE FINANCIAL COST

Divorce also has very tangible costs. If you choose divorce, your finances will be affected for years to come. Divorced parents typically struggle with poverty. This is especially true of the mothers, who experience a 73% decline in their standard of living in the first year after divorce. The poverty rate for children in single parent homes is five times the rate for children living with two parents. [69]

Gary Richmond reports the comments of various divorcees. One said, "My divorce took me from comfort to poverty. I guess it's poverty when you can no longer pay your basic living expenses and you lose all your credit." Another said, "It seems that most of the support from my husband goes to child care so I can work. My hourly wage is low." A third commented, "It was hard to leave our home and move to a rental house. We had to take in boarders to make ends meet." Another one lamented, "It's been hard since the divorce. You can best describe our life as 'no frills.'"[70]

Then there are the actual costs of the divorce: the average couple spends $15,000. Lawyers are the real winners. At $300/hour, the bill adds up quickly. Richmond writes: "The sad truth...you will be paying lawyers by the hour, so it is in their best interest to prolong the proceedings." One woman reported to him that she received a bill from her lawyer for $2,114.00 for one month alone. Her total bill was more than $7,000.00.[71]

THE HEALTH COSTS

Divorce also directly affects one's health in a negative way. Research shows that divorce and separation increases men's cigarette and alcohol consumption, leading to more problem drinking than among married men. For women, divorce and separation decreases their hours of sleep.

In an article entitled, "The Disturbing Facts"[72], the following statements were made:

> 40% - Increased risk of premature death for men and women who go through divorce.
>
> 200% - Increased risk of suicide for divorced men or women.
>
> 300% - Increased risk for divorced or separated men of dying due to cardiovascular disease.
>
> 500% - Increased risk for divorced or separated women of being admitted to a psychiatric facility.
>
> 1000% - Increased risk for divorced or separated men of being admitted to a psychiatric facility.

Another very sad statistic, that I should mention, is that second marriages have less than 30 percent chance of surviving five years or more, and a third marriage has a less than 15 percent chance of survival.[73] Hopefully, these statistics are terrible enough to make those who see divorce as their first option reconsider. Perhaps, as you read this, you are already paying these costs. I pray for you and the challenge it presents.

IS DIVORCE EVER APPROPRIATE?

Someone once asked Ruth Graham, the wife of evangelist Billy Graham, if she believed in divorce. "Divorce?" she responded, "No. *Murder?* Yes! But divorce, no." So far, we have looked at the costs of divorce, but I want to ask a question, "Is divorce ever appropriate?" Is there ever a time when God says it is okay to divorce? There are two passages in the Bible where divorce is spoken about that I want to look at and see if we can find an answer to that question.

JESUS' TEACHING ON DIVORCE

In His famous sermon, usually called the "Sermon on the Mount", Jesus said, "It has been said, 'Anyone who divorces his wife must give her a certificate of divorce'" (Matthew 5:31). Jesus was referring to Deuteronomy 24:1, where Moses instructed the proper procedure when a divorce was planned: "If a man marries a woman who becomes displeasing to him because he finds something indecent about her, and he writes her a certificate of divorce, gives it to her and sends her from his house..." This Law of Moses' was not instituting divorce (it already had been in existence for a long time, even by Moses' time), but rather regulating that which was already instituted by the larger culture around the

Israelites. The point of the Mosaic legislation was that once a man divorced his wife and she remarried, she could never come back to him. Deuteronomy 24:2–4 goes on to say,

> And if after she leaves his house she becomes the wife of another man, and her second husband dislikes her and writes her a certificate of divorce, gives it to her and sends her from his house, or if he dies, then her first husband, who divorced her, is not allowed to marry her again after she has been defiled. That would be detestable in the eyes of the LORD.

A number of years ago, a father came to me for counsel about his daughter's situation. Her husband had divorced her and remarried. Then, he had divorced his second wife and was calling his first wife, this man's daughter, wanting to get back together with her. "What is the right thing for her to do?" the father asked me. My response was that, if nothing else, this passage teaches that once a person remarries to someone else, the first marriage is forever over.

But based on this passage from Deuteronomy, there arose a great debate in the first century over the grounds for divorce. The school of Rabbi Shammai understood that uncleanness ("something indecent" NIV) meant sexual immorality, and said that was the only valid reason for divorce. The school of Rabbi Hillel understood uncleanness to mean any sort of indiscretion, even to the point where burning the breakfast was considered valid grounds for divorce.[74]

That debate was then brought to Jesus by the Pharisees to see what He would say. Matthew 19 records this interaction: "Some Pharisees came to him to test him. They asked, 'Is it lawful for a man to divorce his wife for any and every reason?'" (Matthew 19:3). This had been the position of Rabbi Hillel. Jesus responded with:

> Haven't you read that at the beginning the Creator 'made them male and female,' and said, 'For this reason a man will leave his father and mother and be united to his wife, and the two will become one flesh'? So they are no longer two, but one. Therefore what God has joined together, let man not separate.
> Matthew 19:4–6

Jesus' point was to return to the original intention and purpose of God for marriage as recorded in Genesis 2.

The Pharisees then pursued the matter further: "Why then did Moses command that a man give his wife a certificate of divorce and send her away?" (Matthew 19:7). Jesus went on to give His teaching: "Moses permitted you to divorce your wives because your hearts were hard. But it was not this way from the beginning." The Mosaic Law was a concession to sinful human hearts, not God's divine plan. He went on to say, "I tell you that anyone who divorces his wife, except for marital unfaithfulness, and marries another woman commits adultery" (Matthew 19:8–9).

According to Jesus, the only ground for divorce is sexual immorality. The word that is translated "marital unfaithfulness" in the New International Version is *porneia*, which comes from the Greek word *porne*. We get the English word "pornography" from it. The meaning of *porne* is "prostitute", which itself comes from the root word, *pernummi*, meaning "to sell." The word *porne* simply means "sexual immorality of all sorts," whether it is adultery, homosexuality, lesbianism, bestiality, incest, and so forth. A lady in my church spoke of her daughter-in-law who had become a prostitute. "That qualifies for divorce, doesn't it?" she asked me. "Yes," I said, "Prostitutes are guilty of *'porneia.'*"

The reason that Jesus made sexual immorality permissible grounds for divorce was because He knew that it is sexual immorality, not divorce, which breaks the marriage bond. Because, as we have seen, marriage is "one flesh;" sexual immorality breaks that bond. Therefore divorce is permitted. It is in the intimacy of the immoral sexual act that that one flesh relationship is shattered. Divorce, then, merely recognizes that the one flesh has already been torn apart.

This then is a "Biblical" divorce permitted by God. All other reasons for divorce such as "incompatibility" are sinful and, as such, need to be called just that: "sinful." Up until 1968, the law in Canada, for example, permitted only adultery as the basis of divorce. But then in 1968, it was expanded to include marital breakdown, no matter what. Christians, however, are governed by a higher law than the laws of the country they live in.

You may be wondering, "But what about abuse as a 'cause' for divorce? What about physical or mental abuse? What if a husband is physically beating up his wife? Isn't that a 'cause' for divorce?" Yes, it is a cause, but a "sinful" cause. I will explain more, later.

Now, divorce in cases where *porneia* has occurred is never the first option, but rather the last resort. For Christians who name the name of Christ, divorce is to take place only after all attempts at reconciliation and restoration have been exhausted. In the movie, "Midnight", starring Claudette Colbert and Don Ameche, there is a French law which says that before divorce can be granted, the couple must spend at least 15 minutes in a "reconciliation room." That might not be a bad idea. People spend thousands of dollars on weddings only to have them fall apart because of some misunderstanding. But because divorce is seen as the first option, most never consider reconciliation.

Following *porneia,* the first step is repentance by the offending party and forgiveness by the offended party. I fully recognize the challenge of forgiveness here by the offended party is very great. But I think what Rick Warren says applies very aptly here: "Remember, you will never be asked to forgive someone else more than God has already forgiven you." [75]

In the event either of these parties refuses to do so, the disciplinary steps listed by Jesus in Matthew 18:15–17 need to be taken by the church:

1. Confront in private.

2. Confront with one or two witnesses.

3. Confront before the church.

4. Treat the person as unsaved. Then, and only then, may a Biblical divorce take place.

This is where the issue of abuse in a marriage is dealt with. The abuser is brought to the church elders for discipline of his abuse. He must be disciplined by the church through the undertaking of these four steps in Matthew 18. If he is unresponsive, the final step is to declare him to be the unsaved person he is acting like.

PAUL'S TEACHING ON DIVORCE

Not all of what the Bible teaches on divorce is found in the teachings of Jesus. Some is found in the teaching of the Apostle Paul in 1 Corinthians 7. First, Paul teaches that marriage between two believers is permanent: till death parts. "To the married I give this command (not I, but the Lord): A wife must not separate from her husband" (1 Corinthians 7:10). This is similar to what Paul wrote in Romans 7:2: "By law a married woman is bound to her husband as long as he is alive, but if her husband dies, she is released from the law of marriage."

Some have wondered if Paul's statement of "not I but the Lord" in verse 10 and "I, not the Lord" in verse 12 constitute a concession by him that his word was not the final authoritative word on the matter. But that is not at all what he has in mind. Paul's statement of "not I but the Lord" refers to those aspects of the marriage and divorce that the Lord, Jesus Himself, spoke on while He was on earth and which are found in the gospels. When he says, "I, not the Lord", Paul is saying that this is further, new revelation on topics Jesus did not cover, for whatever reason, while He was on earth. This is not in any way a lowering of the authority of inspired scripture as recorded in 1 Corinthians 7.

Then Paul addresses the issue of what to do when two believers cannot get along together. He says they may separate but not divorce. "But if she does (i.e. separate), she must remain unmarried or else be reconciled to her husband. And a husband must not divorce his wife" (1 Corinthians 7:11). Sometimes due to the hardness of people's hearts, two Christians just cannot get along together, and they do separate. Then they have two options. One is to remain single. One woman who had separated herself from her Christian husband asked her pastor, "What are my options?" Based on this passage, he counseled her, "Remain single."

The other option is for them to reconcile. In the devotional booklet, *Our Daily Bread,* Louis Evans, former pastor of Hollywood Presbyterian Church, said that he never knew a couple who went ahead with a divorce, after first praying together, on their knees every day, for a week.

Now Paul addresses one further situation: the case of a believer who is married to an unbeliever. Many in Corinth had come to Christ as result of the preaching of the gospel, but their spouses had not. What were they to do? Should they divorce their spouses as Ezra had commanded the Israelites in Ezra chapter 10? In that context, we read:

> Then Shecaniah son of Jehiel, one of the descendants of Elam, said to Ezra, 'We have been unfaithful to our God by marrying foreign women from the peoples around us. But in spite of this, there is still hope for Israel. Now let us make a covenant before our God to send away all these women and their children, in accordance with the counsel of my lord and of those who fear the commands of our God. Let it be done according to the Law.
> Ezra 10:2–3

And so they did: "They all gave their hands in pledge to put away their wives, and for their guilt they each presented a ram from the flock as a guilt offering" (Ezra 10:19).

It is here that Paul gives new teaching that Jesus in His earthly ministry had not: "To the rest I say this (I, not the Lord): If any brother has a wife who is not a believer and she is willing to live with him, he must not divorce her. And if a woman has a husband who is not a believer and he is willing to live with her, she must not divorce him" (1 Corinthians 7:12–13). If the unbeliever is "willing" to live with her, she must not divorce him. The word translated "willing" in this passage is translated as "heartily approve" in Romans 1:32. The implication is the unbeliever totally supports the believer in his or her faith in Christ.

One of the major reasons they should not divorce

is because of the spiritual impact he or she can have on their spouse and children. "For the unbelieving husband has been sanctified through his wife, and the unbelieving wife has been sanctified through her believing husband. Otherwise your children would be unclean, but as it is, they are holy" (1 Corinthians 7:14).

My wife's grandmother, for 40 years, endured an incredibly hard marriage. Today, most women would have left such a marriage. I heard her tell Linda of his repeated infidelities, abuse, and such. But she chose to remain in the marriage. Then, shortly before her husband died, he came to Christ largely as result, I believe, of her prayers and her faithful life. I will never forget receiving the phone call telling us of this joyous event and the corroborating evidence of the wholesale change in him. We were told, "You should hear grandpa pray!" I later had a conversation with him myself and he asked me, "Do you think God has forgiven me all of my sins?" I assured him, on the basis of the Word of God, that yes, He had.

But, Paul goes on to allow that if the unbeliever is not willing to live with him/her, they may divorce. "But if the unbeliever leaves, let him do so. A believing man or woman is not bound in such circumstances; God has called us to live in peace" (1 Corinthians 7:15). I recall one fine Christian man sharing how that after he accepted Christ, his wife told him, essentially: "It's either that Jesus or me. Take your pick!" "I take Jesus," he said. As result, she walked out on him. Subsequently, he remarried, this time to a fine Christian woman, and today is serving God in the ministry.

Paul's permission to divorce here is given because, he says, there are no guarantees that by hanging on, the unbeliever will be saved. "How do you know, wife, whether you will save your husband? Or, how do you know, husband, whether you will save your wife?" (1 Corinthians 7:16). The believer is not bound in such a case and may remarry, though only to another believer (1 Corinthians 7: 27–28).

It is here that the case of an abusing husband, who has been dealt with by church discipline, should be mentioned. The fourth step of discipline as earlier mentioned determines that such a man is truly not a believer at all, due to his unwillingness to repent of that sin. At this point, Paul's permission to divorce, and subsequently remarry, applies.

One final comment: people who have divorced for whatever reason, prior to coming to Christ, have that sin of divorce forgiven, just like every other sin they have committed. The sin of divorce is not the unpardonable sin.

CONCLUSION

It is impossible to cover every potential situation in marriage breakdowns, as it affects the topic of divorce: "What about if...?" But these Biblical principles do give some guidance as to how to navigate through the murky waters of marriage break-up.

Having said that, it needs to be reaffirmed that the ultimate goal of marriage is a life-long commitment. Divorce is only the last resort, if need be.

QUESTIONS FOR SMALL GROUP DISCUSSION

1. Give some examples of the high cost of divorce you have seen in other people's marriages. What are some of the costs you have seen the children pay? What have been some of the financial costs incurred? What health costs have there been?

2. What is the one exception where Jesus does permit divorce to take place between two believers? But even in that case, what other steps should have been taken so that divorce is a last resort?

3. What should be done in a marriage where, though there has been no sexual immorality, there has been abuse, use of pornography, or other activities that are very destructive to the marriage relationship? What are the steps that should be taken in a Christian marriage where such things are happening?

4. What are the other grounds for a Biblical divorce that the Apostle Paul grants, according to this chapter? Why should a Christian want to "remain" in such a marriage, if at all possible? And why should a Christian not feel guilty if leaving the marriage is the only option according to Paul?

5. Is divorce the unpardonable sin? Can a person be divorced and still be in a right relationship with God?

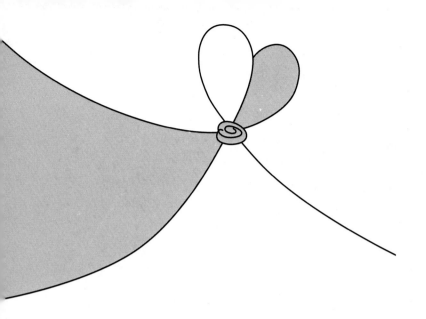

WHEN YOUR HEART IS BREAKING: THE END OF A MARRIAGE

An elderly man lay sick in bed about to die, and his wife sat at his side. He was giving her his final comments. "Sarah," he said, "When we were first married and I fell and broke my leg, you were there with me." He went on to say, "When I later got pneumonia, you were there! And remember the time I got food poisoning? You were there too! And when I had a heart attack, you were there!" He concluded, "Now here on my deathbed, you are with me."

"Sarah, you know what?" he said as he raised himself up on his elbow and looked her in the eye. "You're bad luck!"

There is a famous stress test called the Holmes Rahe Stress Scale.[76] It measures how much stress you can handle in life. If you score over 300 points, it tells you that you are headed for some kind of mental, physical, or emotional breakdown. The top two items in the stress test, interestingly, are: 1) the death of a spouse (100 points) and 2) the divorce from a spouse (73 points). The two things that cause the most stress in life both are related to the end of a marriage.

Every marriage eventually ends; most by death, some prematurely by divorce. Either way, it is a painful and heart breaking experience. How do you handle it?

THE DEATH OF A SPOUSE

The death of a spouse is a difficult, yet a God ordained trial that every couple has to eventually face. Abraham faced it when his beloved wife Sarah died. "Sarah lived to be 127 years old. She died at Kiriath Arba, in the land of Canaan, and Abraham went to mourn for Sarah and to weep over her" (Genesis 23:1–2).

Someone has written, "Love isn't an act; it's a whole life. It's you at 75 and her at 71, each of you listening for the other's step in the next room, each afraid that a sudden silence, a sudden cry could mean a lifetime's talk is over."

Several years ago, I watched my father and mother deal with mom's terminal disease. All of us as children were with them in their home the day we were moving them from the house into a senior's complex. I watched as they walked from room to room, looking at things, and I wondered what memories must have been going through their minds.

In the last few months of mom's life, dad took care of her. He would get up in the middle of the night to make her some food: "I want to eat!" she would plead. She could only eat bread shredded into warm milk due to the tumor growing in her throat. He would feed her as a little child. One of the most moving pictures in my memory is seeing him stand in front of her open coffin at her funeral and with both hands upraised in the air, hearing him cry out, "Good bye, Mary!"

Couples have long said, "I hope you die first." They say that, not to spite but to say, "I want to spare you the pain and heartache of bereavement." Although, I must admit, that is not always the case. I remember reading about one couple who fought constantly. Finally, she came to him and said, "Enough of this fighting already! I'm going to pray that the Lord takes one of us home. And," she continued, "When He does, I'm going to go and live with my sister!"

C.S. Lewis is one of Christianity's finest apologists. His masterpiece is the book, *Mere Christianity*, which made an incredible impact on me when I read it at the age of 21. At the age of 58, in April 1956, Lewis, a confirmed bachelor, married Joy Davidman, an American poet with two small children. After four brief, intensely happy years of marriage, she died of cancer.

Lewis wrote a book entitled, *A Grief Observed* in which he freely confesses his doubts, his rage, and his awareness of human frailty.

In it, he writes, "Meanwhile, where is God? This is one of the most disquieting symptoms. When you are happy, so happy that you have no sense of needing Him, if you turn to Him then with praise, you will be welcomed with open arms. But go to Him when your need is desperate, when all other help is vain and what do you find? A door slammed in your face and a sound of bolting and double bolting on the inside. After that, silence. You may as well turn away."[77] The death of a spouse is a painful and sad experience.

DIVORCE FROM A SPOUSE

The second and even greater shock is that of a divorce. Divorce from a spouse is even more difficult than the death of a spouse because, unlike a death of a spouse, it is not God ordained.

There is an aspect of rejection in divorce that is not found in death. The fact is many people go through a divorce they did not ask for, did not want, did not seek, and which was forced on them. You cannot make somebody fall in love with you, and you cannot make them stay in love with you either. Sometimes it happens.

What do you do when your heart is breaking, when a marriage ends, whether it is by death or divorce? There are six specific actions the Bible speaks about that can help you through this difficult time in your life.[78]

YOU NEED FRIENDS

First, you need some friends who will rally around you and hold you up. "If one person falls, another can reach out and help. But people who are alone when they fall are in real trouble...two can stand back-to-back and conquer. Three are even better" (Ecclesiastes 4:10, 12, NLT). In a crisis, we tend to want to withdraw and to isolate ourselves. Frequently people in pain are embarrassed by their situation and do not want others to know. They want to say, "Everything's cool", knowing all the while everything is not "cool."

Isolation is the exact opposite of what you need. In a crisis, you need friends who will be there with you. "Let us not give up meeting together, as some are in the habit of doing, but let us encourage one another—and all the more as you see the Day approaching" (Hebrews 10:25). Many people have found, in a crisis, that a small group was exceptionally helpful. That is because these people became their support network in that period of time.

Over the years, I have watched many people who come to church. Each Sunday morning, they walk in and walk out but they never get to know anybody. I have frequently said from the pulpit that this is an inadequate way of living the Christian life. If they had a crisis tomorrow, not a single person in the church could help them because no one knows them well enough. They are in a very precarious position.

My recommendation is that if you are reading this

and not yet in a crisis, which by the way is inevitable in your life, that you will begin to develop relationships with mature Christians. You need people who can give you godly, strong advice and who will lovingly, unselfishly care for you when that inevitable time comes. At the same time, they might need you similarly to care for them. When you are in a relationship with them, then you are available also for them. That is the give and take of the Christian life that God planned.

ACCEPT WHAT HAS HAPPENED

Acceptance of what has happened is the second step in finding healing and wholeness after a crisis. The first thing you will have to come to terms with is the fact that you cannot change the past. Whether you try being bitter, worrying, moaning, or having a pity party, none of these will be able to change the past. You have to face reality that, yes, this is a very painful situation, but life has to go on. Acceptance is the second step in finding healing and wholeness after a crisis.

A good example of this is how King David in the Old Testament reacted to the death of his baby child. David had committed adultery with Bathsheba and as result, she had gotten pregnant. Then, to cover up what he had done, he had her husband killed in battle and he married her. After the child was born, it became very sick as result of the judgment of God. You can imagine the mixed emotions David felt about that child, knowing that he had committed both adultery and murder and this was the result.

The Bible tells us that David fasted and prayed for the child to get better, but instead of getting better, it died. When the baby died, David ended his fast and as he ate, his servants questioned him why. He answered, "While the child was still alive, I fasted and wept. I thought, 'Who knows? The LORD may be gracious to me and let the child live.' But now that he is dead, why should I fast? Can I bring him back again? I will go to him, but he will not return to me" (2 Samuel 12:22–23). David accepted what could not be changed.

When a marriage ends, what do you do with your grief? Wallow in self pity? Play the "if only" game? Resign from life? Build a wall of self imposed isolation? No. Like David, we accept reality and what cannot be changed.

CALL OUT TO GOD

People often ask, "Why did God allow it to happen?" Even Job struggled with how God had allowed things to happen in his life as they had: "Why does the Almighty not set times for judgment? Why must those who know him look in vain for such days?" (Job 24:1). When it comes to death, we must realize that every person has a time. "A time to be born and a time to die" is the way Ecclesiastes 3:2 puts it. I am convinced that you will not live a minute longer than what God has planned. The moment you die was the time God had planned for you to die. We are told in Revelation 1:18 that He alone holds the keys of death.

As for the divorce, I am also convinced that God could have stopped it from happening, as He could stop all evil in the world. But here is the problem with Him doing that: in order for Him to have stopped your divorce from happening, He would have to take away everyone's free will. Tell me, how do you feel about losing your free will and becoming a robot or a zombie? For example, next Sunday morning, you wake up and think, "I don't feel like going to church." But all of a sudden you find yourself being lifted out of bed and your hands are putting your clothes on. You are steered towards the door, into your car, which heads right for the church. In the service, when the offering is received, your hand goes into your wallet and pulls out 10% of your weekly income. You get my point. Not much fun, right?

You see, part of the problem of having a free will is that we all often make dumb decisions. Ecclesiastes 7:29 says, "This only have I found: God made mankind upright, but men have gone in search of many schemes." Because of our dumb, and sometimes intentionally evil decisions, innocent people get hurt. Maybe that is you, hurt by your spouse's infidelity and subsequent divorce. And, in all likelihood, you yourself have also hurt others.

So, the divorce happened. But instead of blaming God, why don't you cry out to Him? The Psalmist wrote, "I cry out to the Lord; I plead for his mercy. I pour out my complaints before him and tell him all my troubles. For I am overwhelmed, and you alone know the way I should turn..." (Psalm 142:1–2, 6, NLT). Tell God how you feel. Receive the comfort He has promised: "The Lord is close to the brokenhearted and saves those who are crushed in spirit" (Psalm 34:18). "He heals the brokenhearted and binds up their wounds" (Psalm 147:3).

Whatever your crisis, God is willing to help. He understands feelings of hurt, rejection, frustration, and pain. In Matthew 11:28, Jesus says, "Come to me, all you who are weary and burdened, and I will give you rest."

LISTEN TO GOD

Often when you are in a crisis, you cannot think straight. Even the Psalmist admitted that was his case: "When my heart was grieved and my spirit embittered, I was senseless and ignorant; I was a brute beast before you" (Psalm 73:21–22). When Linda was in labor about to give birth to our first born son, I was there in the delivery room with her to help her. I remember her asking me, "Please rub my back!" And so I did. But just as I put my hand on her back, she screamed out, "Don't touch me!" Needless to say, I was confused. But I realized that due to the stress of the moment, she was not reacting normally. In crisis, you do not make smart decisions.

One of the realities of going through a crisis is that our moods go up and down continually. We fluctuate all over the place: one minute we are thinking, *Yes, I can make it through this!* and the next minute we are thinking, *There is absolutely no way that I can make it!* Those of you who have gone through a divorce, will know that one minute you are saying, "I hate all men/women!" and the next one, you are saying, "Give me a man/woman!" Our emotions are all over the place.

That is why you need the stabilizing factor of God's Word. You need to read it and saturate your mind with it because, while your moods are going flip-flop, it stands the same. It has been true for 2000 years. The Bible is the greatest antidote to depression. "I am completely discouraged...Revive me by your word," said the Psalmist (Psalm 119:25, TLB).

Some people find that when they are going through a crisis, they do not sleep very well. They keep on thinking about their crisis, their mind is in overdrive and it just will not shut down at night. So what do you do when you cannot sleep at night in a crisis? Sit up and watch TV infomercials or "Nick at Night"? I would not recommend that. The Psalmist said he coped with his pain in the night hours by going to God's word: "I stay awake through the night, thinking about your promises" (Psalm 119:148 TLB).

ASK FOR FORGIVENESS

A main problem people face when relationships break down is to go to one of two extremes: "It's all your fault" or "It's all my fault"—both extremes are wrong. In every relationship, there are legitimate reasons for both resentment and guilt. People hurt you, and you hurt them.

First, deal with your part of the problem. Begin by confessing your sinful actions to God and asking His forgiveness. Ultimately all sin is against Him. After David committed adultery with Bathsheba and had her husband killed in the subsequent cover up, he was mightily convicted over what he had done. In his penitential prayer in Psalm 51, he said, "Against you, you only, have I sinned and done what is evil in your sight" (Verse 4). David saw that His sin had offended a just and holy God, most of all.

Say to Him, "God, this is my part in ending this marriage. This is what I did wrong." David prayed, "Have mercy on me, O God, according to your unfailing love; according to your great compassion blot out my transgressions. Wash away all my iniquity and cleanse me from my sin" (Psalm 51:1–2). In another Psalm, he put it, "My guilt overwhelms me—it is a burden too heavy to bear...But I confess my sins; I am deeply sorry for what I have done" (Psalm 38:4, 18, NLT). Then, humble yourself and go to the other person and ask their forgiveness. "Confess your sins to each other..." is the excellent advice of James 5:16.

OFFER FORGIVENESS

Second, offer forgiveness. "Get rid of all bitterness... forgiving each other just as in Christ God forgave you" (Ephesians 4:31–32). There is no more important step to take when your heart is breaking, particularly after a divorce, than the step of forgiveness. "Do not seek revenge or bear a grudge against one of your people, but love your neighbor as yourself. I am the Lord" (Leviticus 19:18).

The person who refuses to forgive brings tremendous personal bondage into his life. Most unforgiveness begins with being hurt by someone else. The hurt leads to anger, which in turn leads to bitterness and ultimately to an unforgiving spirit. But the act of refusing to forgive is actually a form of revenge. We think, *She hurt me, I'll hurt her back; I won't forgive her!"*

But an unforgiving spirit glues us to our painful past through our memories. It is like a bungee cord in our minds that is attached to the event. It dooms us to relive the pain every time we remember it because every time we remember it, we hurt all over again. The bungee cord of memory yanks that painful memory of the past back against us and slams us in the face.

Another illustration of that is like a videotape planted in the soul. As you watch the initial painful experience being replayed through your memory, you feel the pain again and again.

An unforgiving spirit is a revenge that exacts a high toll from us. "Resentment kills a fool" (Job 5:2). It has been said, "Bitterness is the poison we swallow, while hoping the other person dies." It is like the old comedy routine with Amos and Andy. Andy sees Amos with a bottle of nitroglycerin around his neck and asks him why he is wearing it. Amos says, "Remember how old

Joe is always tapping me on the chest when he's talking to me? I'm fed up with it! The next time he does, he's going to blow off his finger!"

The person who refuses to forgive also brings himself into bondage to Satan. An unforgiving spirit is like opening the door of your life and inviting Satan in. Awhile ago, rock star, Marilyn Manson, was in Toronto, and at the conclusion of his concert, gave an altar call for people to come forward and accept Satan. For true Christians, such a thing horrifies them, yet many will do exactly the same thing when they refuse to forgive those who have offended them.

In his book, *Bondage Breaker,* Neil Anderson writes, "Unforgiveness is the number one avenue Satan uses to gain entrance into the believer's life. It is an open invitation to Satan's bondage in our lives."[79] That's why the apostle Paul writes, "What I have forgiven…I have forgiven in the sight of Christ for your sake, in order that Satan might not outwit us. For we are not unaware of his schemes" (2 Corinthians 2:10–11). Satan's scheme is to get you into his bondage through your unforgiving spirit.

But when we forgive, we experience personal freedom. Again, Neil Anderson writes, "Forgiveness is not something we do for others…it is something you do for yourself…You don't forgive someone for their sake; you do it for your sake so you can be free…Your need to forgive is not an issue between you and the offender, it's between you and God."[80]

Lewis Smedes puts it this way: "To forgive is to put

down your 50 pound pack after a 10 mile climb up a mountain; to forgive is to fall into a chair after a 26 mile marathon; to forgive is to set a prisoner free and to discover that the prisoner was you!"[81]

You experience freedom from the painful past. I said earlier that an unforgiving spirit glues us to our painful past through our memories. The question: "How do you stop the pain?" The answer: the act of forgiveness stops the pain. You stop the cycle of unfair pain turning in your mind by forgiving the person who hurt you. By forgiving, you snap the bungee cord of memory; you pull the cord on the VCR of the soul and stop the videotape of the past.

Forgiveness also frees you from having to get revenge. In the book of Genesis, Joseph is sold into slavery to Egypt by his 10 older brothers who hate him. There, in Egypt, Joseph rises to become Prime Minister and in that position, saves his family from starvation. But his brothers fearfully wonder, after their father Jacob dies, "What if Joseph holds a grudge against us and pays us back for all the wrong we did to him?" When Joseph hears that, he reassures them: "Don't be afraid! Am I in the place of God? You intended to harm me, but God intended it for good to accomplish what is now being done: the saving of many lives!" (Genesis 50:15, 19–20). Joseph was essentially saying, "Vengeance is God's job, not mine."

When people who have been deeply hurt hear that, they say, "But that's not fair! Why should I let them off the hook?" I like Neil Anderson's answer to that objection: "That's precisely the problem! You are hooked to them, still bound by your past."[82] And so you keep on hurting. As someone has said, "The person who suffers most is not the perpetrator: it's the one who refuses to forgive." The person who hurt you likely has forgotten all about the event; they have moved on. But it is you who stews on and hurts on.

When you forgive them, you let them off your hook. But, let me assure you, they are never off of God's. He will deal with them fairly; something you cannot do! "Do not take revenge, my friends, but leave room for God's wrath. For it is written, 'Vengeance is mine; I will repay', says the Lord" (Romans 12:19). I always tell people, "Judgment is still ahead, not behind us."

When we forgive, we also find freedom from Satan and his control of us. As we forgive others, we close the doors to him in our lives. Paul urged the Corinthians to forgive an offending brother in their midst, "in order that Satan might not outwit us," he wrote, "for we are not unaware of his schemes" (2 Corinthians 2:11).

Question: How do I forgive someone? Realize that forgiveness is a choice, an act of the will. As the experience of unforgiveness begins with a hurt, so also the experience of forgiveness begins with the decision to forgive. "If your brother sins, rebuke him, and if he sins against you seven times in a day, and seven times comes back to you and says, 'I repent', forgive him" (Luke 17:3–4).

People often say to me, "But I can't forgive! You don't know how much that person hurt me!" My response is always, "I agree. I probably don't know how much that person hurt you. But we *can* forgive. Since forgiveness is something that God requires of us, it is something we can do. He would never ask us to do something we could never do."

Simply pray to God aloud, "Father, I forgive (name the person) for (name the offence)." What you will experience is a freedom and joy you never dreamed possible. Do not worry about your feelings initially, however, because that comes later. The important thing is experiencing the freedom from bondage to an unforgiving spirit.

I shared this truth in a message in Vancouver a few years ago. Six months later, I was at a conference in Edmonton and a lady in her 70's came up to me and said, "You were in our church six months ago and you announced your sermon title, 'The Freedom of Forgiveness'. I remember thinking, 'This will be good for so and so…' And I took out a pen to take notes. But God spoke to me and said, 'No, Olive. This is for you.' He showed me someone I hadn't forgiven for something they had done to me 40 years ago! So, I forgave that person and do you know what, pastor? I haven't been depressed since!"

Later in that conference, I met that woman's pastor and told him what she had said to me. "Oh, yes, that has been so amazing!" he responded. "For 40 years, she has been under such a cloud of depression that she was unable to get out of bed most mornings. But since she forgave, she is like a new person!"

That is the freedom of forgiveness. If you have been divorced, you may need to forgive more than just your spouse. You may have to forgive some cruel in-laws, some self-righteous friends, people who did not support you or the person who stole your mate. But, I urge you, forgive them.

KEEP FOCUSING ON GOD'S PLAN FOR YOUR LIFE

Many people in crisis feel that there is no hope. David wrote, "I would have despaired unless I had believed that I'd see the goodness of the LORD..." (Psalm 27:13, NASB). Realize God still loves you—He has a plan for your life and He is not finished with you. "God who began the good work within you will keep right on helping you grow in his grace until his task within you is finally finished..." (Philippians 1:6, TLB).

The one thing you do not do is jump right into a new relationship. That is the last thing you need right now. Earlier, I pointed out that there is a greater failure rate for second marriages than there are for first marriages. Why? People get in a hurry and, either because of financial or sexual pressure or because of loneliness or some other reason; they jump into a new relationship before they have been healed. That is not going to solve your pain. You need to look to God and get healed first.

Even after the death of a spouse, I believe you need at least two years of grieving before you think of remarriage. Instead, focus on becoming the person God wants you to become. "Put your heart right, reach out to God...then face the world again, firm and courageous. Then all your troubles will fade from your memory..." (Job 11:13–16, GN).

One of the most important questions you need to ask yourself, if you find yourself single again by divorce or death is, "What does God want me to learn from all that I have gone through?" Scripture says, "God sometimes uses sorrow in our lives to help us turn away from sin and seek salvation" (2 Corinthians 7:10, NLT).

Some time ago, a fellow I knew went through the shattering experience of losing his wife through divorce. As result of it, he began coming to church, and I was there to help him walk through the pain. After some time, he wrote me a note telling me of his experiences and what he had learned. He gave me his permission to share what he had written with others. He wrote:

> In spite of the incredibly overwhelming and persistent emotional pain I have endured over the past two and a half years of separation from my wife and sons, I am eternally grateful to God for what He has taught me and continues to teach me. In fact, I realize that it was only because of this pain, that I was able to learn some incredible things about people, relationships, and myself. He has taught me a new sensitivity towards people. He has taught me that people are more important than material things. I am continuing to learn about and become more sensitive to these issues. Although on the surface, I do

not appreciate the feeling of pain, I must admit that this was necessary for me to change. In short, I am thankful to God for four things in this regard: 1) The presence of pain. 2) The sensitivity to feel this pain. 3) The ability to recognize and acknowledge this pain as the result of something that is "wrong" or "broken." 4) The ability to embrace and learn from this pain, change something and thereby create the potential for the pain to subside.

That is some of the good that can happen as result of a broken heart after the end of a marriage.

QUESTIONS FOR SMALL GROUP DISCUSSION

1. Tell of some marriages that you have seen end, whether by death or divorce, where it didn't end well. Why did that happen? What factors brought about the unhappy ending?

2. Why is a divorce a more difficult way for a marriage to end than the death of a spouse?

3. Why do people tend to isolate themselves in a crisis? How can friends help?

4. Why is acceptance such a crucial thing in the after-

math of a death of a spouse or the divorce from a spouse?

5. What do you say to someone who's been through either the death or divorce of a spouse who asks, "Why didn't God stop it from happening?"

6. What ways does listening to God in such times help?

7. Discuss the problems caused by an unforgiving spirit and also what the benefits of offering forgiveness are.

8. Why is "What does God want me to learn from all I have gone through?" one of the most important questions one can ask after a death or a divorce?

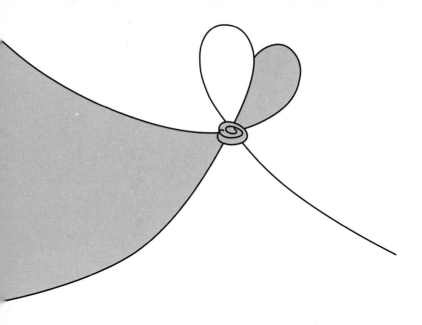

KEEPING THE HOME FIRES BURNING

Back in the days before fire was readily available, villages had people who were given the job of "keepers of the fire." They were charged with the responsibility of keeping the village fire going. People would come to the village fire with their torches, light them and take the fire home with them. This is one of the purposes of this book: I am being a "keeper of the fire" and so helping you to keep your "home fires" burning.

Most marriages begin with great hope for the future. Watch any young couple, how they hold hands, talk, look at each other. Yet, the sad reality is that many of these will experience marital failures down the road.

As I stated before, the average length of marriage now is 12 years.

Peter Drucker, the management guru says, "The longer a company is in business, the more it tends to drift from its original mission." While God has a plan for every family, so does Satan. In these last days, his plan is to drive a wedge between husbands and wives, between parents and children. As the last book in the Bible predicts, Satan will pull out all stops: "Woe to the earth and the sea, because the devil has gone down to you! He is filled with fury, because he knows that his time is short" (Revelation 12:12). Every divorce, every broken home is a victory, a success for him. To counter that, we need, as families, to work hard at keeping the home fires burning.

STOKING THE FLAME OF HONOR

Romans 12:10 says "Love each other with genuine affection and take delight in honoring each other." (NLT) It will be as we concentrate on honoring each other in the family, that we will keep the home fires burning bright.

A group of young children was asked, "What does love mean?" Their answers are insightful. Rebecca, age eight, said, "When my grandmother got arthritis, she couldn't bend over and paint her toenails anymore. So my grandfather did it for her all the time, even when his hands got arthritis too. That's love." Danny, age seven, added, "Love is when my mommy makes coffee for my daddy and she takes a sip before giving it to him, to make sure the taste is okay." Tommy, age six, responded, "Love is like a little old woman and a little old man who are still friends even after they know each other so well." Chris, age eight, gave his version: "Love is when mommy sees daddy smelly and sweaty and still says he is handsomer than Robert Redford."

Let me share with you some practical suggestions for ways to honor. First, show affection. In Song of Solomon 2:6, the beloved says of her lover, "His left arm is under my head, and his right arm embraces me." In our marriages and in our families, we need to show affection to each other. That includes physical affection like holding hands, hugging, and touching. It also includes eye contact and smiling at each other.

As I was recently flying home from a trip, I was given a paper on the plane. In it was an article entitled, "Don't roll your eyes." It said, "'A wealth of research has helped scientists discern what qualities lead to a lasting marriage or divorce,' writes Tara Parker-Pope in *The Wall Street Journal*. 'For instance, research shows eye-rolling after a spouse's comment can be a powerful predictor for divorce.'" So, showing honor to your spouse means not rolling your eyes as they speak.

Honoring your spouse also includes expressing appreciation to them. Husbands should show appreciation to their wives for all they do around the house. In a Bryn Mawr College survey, they discovered that "the average urban woman spends over 80 hours a week at duties about the home."[83] Wayne Dehoney asks, "What man has ever been honest enough to propose to a girl by saying, 'Would you be willing to work for 80 hours a week for me for nothing? Will you wash 150,000 cubic feet of soiled dishes for me just for love? Or will you wash and iron the clothes on a line 47 miles long with two extra miles of specialty items added for each baby? Or will you climb to the top of the Washington Monument for me 12,000 times?' Yet this is the measure of the actual physical work a woman does in the home."[84]

In Proverbs 31, we have the well known chapter on the "Excellent Wife", with all her amazing virtues and talents and accomplishments listed in it. But, I think, the key for this woman's success is in her husband's attitude and statements to her. Note what he says to her in verse 29: "Many women do noble things, but you surpass them all." He was honoring her as he said those things to and about her.

Express your appreciation verbally and in written form. Write love notes to each other on an occasional basis. I will never forget taking a trip to a conference in Chicago, in March of 1973. This was the first time I had been away from Linda for such a long time. When I got there, I was thrilled to discover a little note in the suitcase from Linda: "Your baby daughter says to say hi to daddy..." (She was about seven months pregnant at the time. As it happened, our "baby daughter" turned out to be a big bouncing boy we called "Craig"...) But it meant so much to me.

STOKING THE FLAME OF ENJOYMENT

Proverbs 5:18–19 says, "May your fountain be blessed, and may you rejoice in the wife of your youth...May you ever be captivated by her love." The New Century Version translates it this way: "Be happy with the wife you married when you were young. She gives you joy, as your fountain gives you water. She is as lovely and graceful as a deer. Let her love always make you happy; let her love always hold you captive." God's will is that every home be a place of enjoyment for husbands and wives.

One of the ways to enjoy each other is to have a regular date night. Doug Fields says, "Date each other. When you say 'I do' at the altar, many times you say 'I don't' to dating. We think dating is childish and just for kids. No, it's not. If you want a deep relationship, intimacy and connectedness you have to have those shared experiences. Dating enriches lives. It gives us something to look forward to. It models marriage to our kids. It creates positive memories."[85]

Do fun things together. Linda and I like to go cruising in the 1966 classic Mustang that I have restored. She likes to ride and I like to drive the car! Each summer, we take a day off and go along a favourite drive that includes a tea house where we stop for lunch. It is always fun.

If need be, cut back on other activities to give you time to do so. Max Lucado writes,

> Busyness is an expert in robbing the sparkle and

replacing it with the drab. Busyness invented the yawn and put the hum in the humdrum. The strategy of busyness is deceptive. With the passing of time, he'll infiltrate your heart with fatigue and cover the cross with dust so you'll be safely out of reach of change. Busyness won't steal your marriage from you. He'll do something far worse. He'll paint it with the familiar coat of drabness. He'll replace evening gowns with bathrobes, nights on the town with evenings in the recliner and romance with routine. He'll scatter the dust of yesterday over the wedding pictures in the hallway until they become a memory of another couple in another time. Hence, walks won't be taken, games will go unplayed, hearts will go unnurtured, and opportunities for intimacy will go ignored, all because the poison of busyness has blinded your eyesight to the wonder of your spouse.[86]

Laugh together. Psalms 126:2 says, "Our mouths were filled with laughter, our tongues with songs of joy. Then it was said among the nations, 'The LORD has done great things for them.'" Happy couples do a lot of laughing together. "A cheerful heart is good medicine, but a crushed spirit dries up the bones" (Proverbs 17:22).

STOKING THE FLAME OF SERVANTHOOD

In Matthew 20:25–26, Jesus said to His disciples, "You know that the rulers of the Gentiles lord it over them, and their high officials exercise authority over them. Not so with you. Instead, whoever wants to become great among you must be your servant." When we place the highest priority on serving our spouse, we will keep the home fires burning the brightest.

There are many ways to serve. Look for opportunities: surprise her by doing something for her. Romans 15:1–2 tells us we are "not to please ourselves. Each of us should please his neighbor for his good, to build him up." Look around. Is there something your spouse does around the house that you could do for them? Guys, if in your home, your wife washes the dishes, go wash the dishes for her. She may pass out, but when she comes to, she will be thrilled. Gals, buy him some batteries for his remote. He'll be really impressed! Look for an opportunity to serve each other.

Here is a practical challenge: look for at least one opportunity each day where you can serve your spouse. You will see plenty of them. I will never forget the day my wife came to my office at Friday noon and picked me up. She did not tell me where we were going; she just drove. We drove into the city of Winnipeg, had coffee and a donut at Robin's Donuts. Then we drove to a downtown hotel parking garage. She opened the trunk of the car which had a suitcase packed for an overnight stay and said, "We're staying here for the weekend as a celebration of your achieving your Master's degree!" It was one of the happiest weekends of my life.

Sid Woodruff tells how his dad used to fall asleep in front of the TV and he was doing the same thing. Then one January 1st, he unplugged the TV and put it in the attic. It was the day of all the college bowl games. But it was his way of saying, "I need to put my family first. I need to serve them."

Some of you may be thinking, "What if I do all the serving and he/she doesn't do any back?" Then you will be just like Jesus. You are never more like Jesus than when you serve, even when you are being mistreated. Do something for him/her that you wouldn't normally do. Let me give you an example: Ladies, what is something that you wouldn't normally do that your husband would enjoy? Watching sports? I don't think that is the first choice of a lot of women. So, go up to him and say, "Let's watch Sports Center together!" He'll love it. That is part of serving.

Guys, what is something we normally wouldn't do that our wives would really like? Allow me to make a suggestion: Go up to her and tell her, "Honey, I would just love to go shopping!" And not at Best Buy or Home Depot, either. I'm thinking of places like the mall. That is not a typical guy thing, right? But *very* desirable for women. Right? Right.

"This is how we know what love is: Jesus Christ laid down his life for us. And we ought to lay down our lives for our brothers...Dear children, let us not love with words or tongue but with actions and in truth" (1 John 3:16, 18).

CONCLUSION

At the beginning of this chapter, I talked about the love

we often see among dating couples and newlyweds. That is how it starts out. Here is how it should end:

"There will come a time when the unthinkable happens, when the aging process will catch up with them and one partner will drop the other off, or check the other one in, at a hospital. That other partner will drive away, kind of knowing in the pit of their stomach that their spouse isn't coming home. The grim reality will be that they've slept together for the last time in one another's arms and the end is near."

"That person will go home and sit in the family room and be filled with memories and remember the first date and the first kiss, the wedding and the honeymoon, the first apartment, the first home, the first child, the first graduation, the first tuition bill. He or she will remember the 25th wedding anniversary and the first grandchild, the retirement party and the last anniversary together. He/she will remember the last kiss."

"Then, that one partner will realize, maybe more fully than ever before how blessed he or she was to have a soul mate for life…To have had a life-long partner who did the whole race together, just like God had envisioned it, just like the Holy Spirit had been rooting them on the entire time, all life long, one run from the starting line to the finish line, all the way to the end together." As someone has put it, "Love starts with a smile, grows with a kiss and ends with a tear."

Unfortunately, there will be those who will sit in that family room on that "final day," filled with remorse. There will be memories of the mistakes they have made in their relationship, memories that will bring them regret. For most of you who have finished reading this book, the good news is that you still have the opportunity to turn your relationship into what God intended it to be. The keys to success in that are what I have written in this book, based on God's word, the Bible.

The memories you will have in that final stage of your life may depend on the decision that you make today. The choice, of course, is yours. One thing we can be sure of is that, by His grace, God will forgive you of your past mistakes. It is what we do from now on that counts.

This is why I wrote this book. It is God's design for how to stay in love, how to keep the home fires burning, how to be "knot happy."

QUESTIONS FOR SMALL GROUP DISCUSSION

1. Discuss practical ways in which any couple can love and honor each other.

2. Talk about why physical affection such as holding hands, hugging, and touching are so important.

3. Discuss things like eye contact and smiling, not rolling the eyes, verbal expressions of appreciation, compliments, and writing love notes. Give reasons why each of these are so crucial. List other means we can show love and honor to each other.

4. How important is a regular date night for a marriage's success? Why should a couple make the effort to do fun things together? How can you stop busyness from robbing you of those times?

5. Discuss ways of serving your spouse. What are some things you have done in the past that made you a servant to him/her? What about guys going to the mall with their wives or gals watching Sports Centre with their husbands? Is that realistic?

6. What should you begin doing today so that someday when this grand thing called marriage is finally over for you, you will look back with joy and gladness at it and not with sadness and regret?

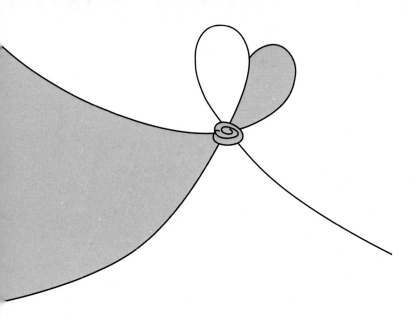

EPILOGUE

Thank you for reading this book. I sincerely hope that reading it has been a helpful experience to you, no matter where you are in your life journey, married or not. My sincere desire has been to glorify God and to help people better know God and His plans for their life. If that has happened to you, my mission has been accomplished. I encourage you to keep on keeping on. If I never meet you on earth, I hope I will meet you in Heaven someday.

Dr. Henry A. Ozirney

ENDNOTES

1 http://www.phrases.org.uk/meanings/382400.html. (accessed January 24, 2007).

2 Nash, Odgen. "I do, I will, I have." Free Poetry E-book: 119 *Poems of Odgen Nash*. www.poemhunter.com/i/ebooks/pdf/ogden_nash_2004_9.pdf (accessed January 24, 2007).

3 House of Commons of Canada, Bill C-38, first reading, February 1, 2005, www2.parl.gc.ca/HousePublications/Publication.aspx?Docid=2333931&file=4 (accessed January 24, 2007).

4 Adams, Jay. *Marriage, Divorce and Remarriage in the Bible*. New Jersey: Presbyterian and Reformed Publishing Company, 1980.

5 Bobby Vinton. "Mr. Lonely," http://www.bobbyvinton.com/lyrics/song5.htm (accessed January 24, 2007).

6 Adams, Jay. *Marriage, Divorce and Remarriage in the Bible*. New Jersey: Presbyterian and Reformed Publishing Company, 1980.

7 pers. comm.)

8 Rogers, Richard and Oscar Hammerstein. "Some Enchanted Evening." http://www.guntheranderson.com/v/data/someench.htm (accessed January 24, 2007).

9 Bono, U2, http://www.sing365.com/music/lyric.nsf/A-Man-And-A-Woman-lyrics-U2/4F73F1112F2ECF0C48256F2000063DDF. (accessed February 7, 2007).

10 Alcorn, Randy. "Deterring Immorality by Counting Its

Cost: The exorbitant price of sexual sin." www.epm.org/articles/leadpur2.html, (accessed January 24, 2007).

11 I heard this on a tape of Chuck Swindoll's message on marriage that had been given to me by a friend.

12 McQuilken, Robertson. "Ministry or Family: The Choice." *Leadership magazine.* Spring Quarter, 1991.

13 http://www.brainyquote.com/quotes/authors/j/j_paul_getty.html (accessed January 26, 2007).

14 Hendricks, Howard. *Heaven Help the Home!* Wheaton: Victor Books, 1973.

15 Ten Boom, Corrie. *The Hiding Place.* Minneapolis: Worldwide Pictures, 1972.

16 Dobson, James. *What Wives Wish Their Husbands Knew About Women.* Wheaton: Tyndale House Publishers, 1988.

17 Lightfoot, Gordon. "If You Could Read My Mind." www.guntheranderson.com/v/data/ifyoucou.htm (accessed January 24, 2007).

18 Chapman, Gary. *The Five Love Languages.* Chicago: Northfield Publishing, 2004.

19 "Romantic love 'lasts just a year.'" BBC News. November 28, 2005. http://news.bbc.co.uk/1/hi/health/4478040.stm (accessed January 24, 2007).

20 Ibid.

21 Sproul, R.C. *In Search of Dignity.* Venture: Regal Books, 1983.

22 Trobisch, Walter. *I Loved a Girl.* San Fransisco:Harper Collins, 1989.

23 Petersen, J. Allen. *The Myth of the Greener Grass.* Wheaton: Tyndale House Publishers, 1983.

24 Patty, Sandi. "Love will be our home." www.lyricsandsongs.com/song/637031.html. (accessed January 27, 2007).

25 Chapman, Gary. Ibid.

26 Jaret, Peter. "The Healing Power of Touch." *Reader's Digest.*

27 Satir, Virginia. http://www.lifepositive.com/Mind/personal-growth/hug/hug-therapy.asp.

28 Smalley, Gary and John Trent. *The Language of Love*. Pomona: Focus on the Family Publishing, 1988.

29 McBride, Cathy. "Touch: the forgotten sense." *Ministry*, November 1988.

30 Chapman, Gary. Ibid. loc cit

31 LaHaye, Tim. *How to be Happy Though Married*. Wheaton: Tyndale House Publishers, 1973.

32 Warren, Rick. "When You've Married The Wrong Person." (sermon, Saddleback Community Church, September 7, 1997).

33 Ibid.

34 Dobson, James. "Focus on the Family Newsletter" Aug. 9,1985.

35 *The Confessions of St. Augustine*. Pocket Books, Inc. Cardinal Edition, 1951.

36 Larson, Bob. *Larson's Book of Cults Branhamism*. Wheaton: Tyndale House Publishers, 1989.

37 Warren, Rick. "Fanning the Flames of Romance" (sermon, Saddleback Community Church, September 21, 1997).

38 Ibid.

39 Ibid.

40 William R. Mattox Jr. "Church Ladies Enjoy Sex More." Amy Writing Awards, 2003 The Amy Foundation: Lansing Michigan.

41 Ibid.

42 Ibid.

43 "Letter to Marie Bonaparte," as quoted in *Sigmund Freud: Life and Work* (1955). Ernest Jones, Vol. 2, Pt. 3, Ch. 16.

44 Fields, Doug. "How to Stay in Love" (sermon Saddleback Community Church, October 5, 1997).

45 Warren, Rick. "Fanning the Flames of Romance" (sermon, Saddleback Community Church, September 21, 1997).

46 www.lyricsfreak.com/h/huey+lewis+and+the+news/mother+in+law_20066258.html (accessed Jan.26/07).

47 Taylor, LaTonya. "The Church of O," *Christianity Today.* April 2, 2002.

48 Warren, Rick. "How to avoid a financial collapse." (sermon, Saddleback Community Church, January 24, 1999).

49 Ibid.

50 http://whatretirement.typepad.com/what_retirement/2005/01/american_demogr.html.

51 Ibid.

52 Ibid.

53 Pascal, Blasé. *Pensees and Other Writings,* trans. Honor Levi. Oxford: Oxford University Press, 1995.

54 *The Confessions of St. Augustine.* Pocket Books, Inc. Cardinal Edition, 1951.

55 Warren, Rick. "Pull Together When You're Pulled Apart." (sermon, Saddleback Community Church, September 14, 1997).

56 Tournier, Paul. *To Understand Each Other.* Atlanta: John Knox Press, 1996.

57 Warren, Rick. "Pull together when you're pulled apart" (sermon, Saddleback Community Church, September 14, 1997).

58 (Hart, Archibald, pers. Comm.)

59 Rowland Croucher (GRID, Winter 1990) http://jmm.aaa.net.au/articles/8108.htm.

60 Warren, Rick. "Pull together when you're pulled apart" (sermon, Saddleback Community Church, September 14, 1997).

61 St. Francis of Assisi. "Prayer of St. Francis" www.prayerguide.org.uk/stfrancis.htm.

62 Warren, Rick. "Pull together when you're pulled apart" (sermon, Saddleback Community Church, September 14, 1997).

63 Warren, Rick. "Marriage Matters" (sermon, Saddleback Community Church, September 14, 1997).

64 Blosser, John. *The National Enquirer.*

65 Medvid, Diane. *The Case Against Divorce.* New York: Donald I. Fine, Inc, 1989.

66 Richmond, Gary. *Focus on the Family,* August 1989.

67 "Free to Be Family." *Focus on the Family.* April 1992. Family Research Council, a division of Focus on the Family.

68 Ibid.

69 Ibid.

70 Richmond, Gary. *Focus on the Family.* August 1989.

71 Ibid.

72 Sources: 1. *Psychosocial and Behavioral Predictors of Longevity: the Aging and death of the termite Friedman.* et. al. American Psychologist, February, 1995 2. *The Costly Consequences of Divorce.* David Larson, Ph.D., National Institute for Healthcare Research, Rockville, MD. September 1995 3. *Marital Disruption as Stressor: A Review and Analysis.* B.R. Bloom, S. J. Asher, S.W. White (1978) Psychological Bulletin, 85, 867–894.

73 Richmond, Gary. *Focus on the Family.* August 1989.

74 Guzik, David. http://www.enduringword.com/commentaries/4019.htm 2004.

75 Warren, Rick. *The Purpose Driven Life.* Grand Rapids: Zondervan, 2002.

76 http://www.geocities.com/beyond_stretched/holmes.htm.

77 Lewis, C.S. *A Grief Observed.* San Francisco: Harper, 2001.

78 Warren, Rick. "When a Marriage Ends." (sermon, Saddleback Community Church, September 28, 1997).

79 Anderson, Neil. *The Bondage Breaker.* Eugene: Harvest House Publishers, 1990.

80 Ibid.

81 Smedes, Lewis. "Forgiveness: The Power to Change the Past," *Christianity Today.* Jan. 7, 1993.

82 Anderson, Neil. *The Bondage Breaker.* Eugene: Harvest House Publishers, 1990.

83 Dehoney, Wayne. *Homemade Happiness.* Nashville: Broadman Press, 1963.

84 Ibid.

85 Fields, Doug. "How to Stay in Love" (sermon, Saddleback Community Church, Lake Forest, California, October 5, 1997).

86 Fields, Doug. "How to Stay in Love" (sermon Saddleback Community Church, Lake Forest, California, October 5, 1997).